...the Super Source®
Tangrams

ETA/Cuisenaire®
Vernon Hills, IL

D1511979

ETA/Cuisenaire® extends its warmest thanks to the many teachers and students across the country who helped ensure the success of the Super Source® series by participating in the outlining, writing, and field testing of the materials.

Project Director: Judith Adams
Managing Editor: Doris Hirschhorn
Editorial Team: John Nelson, Deborah J. Slade, Harriet Slonim, Linda Dodge, Patricia Kijak Anderson
Field Test Coordinator: Laurie Verdeschi

Design Manager: Phyllis Aycock
Text Design: Amy Berger, Tracey Munz
Line Art and Production: Joan Lee, Fiona Santoianni
Cover Design: Michael Muldoon
Illustrations: June Otani

the Super Source® Tangrams Grades 5–6
ISBN 1-57452-017-2
ETA 015137

ETA/Cuisenaire • Vernon Hills, IL 60061-1862
800-445-5985 • www.etacuisenaire.com

Printed in the United States of America.

6 7 8 9 10 11 12   10 09 08 07 06 05

the Super Source
Table of Contents

Using the Super Source®

The Super Source® is a series of books, each of which contains a collection of activities to use with a specific math manipulative. Driving **the Super Source** is ETA/Cuisenaire's conviction that children construct their own understandings through rich, hands-on mathematical experiences. Although the activities in each book are written for a specific grade range, they all connect to the core of mathematics learning that is important to every K-6 child. Thus, the material in many activities can easily be refocused for children at other grade levels. Because the activities are not arranged sequentially, children can work on any activity at any time.

The lessons in **the Super Source** all follow a basic structure consistent with the vision of mathematics teaching described in the *Curriculum and Evaluation Standards for School Mathematics* published by the National Council of Teachers of Mathematics.

All of the activities in this series involve Problem Solving, Communication, Reasoning, and Mathematical Connections—the first four NCTM Standards. Each activity also focuses on one or more of the following curriculum strands: Number, Geometry, Measurement, Patterns/Functions, Probability/Statistics, Logic.

HOW LESSONS ARE ORGANIZED

At the beginning of each lesson, you will find, to the right of the title, both the major curriculum strands to which the lesson relates and the particular topics that children will work with. Each lesson has three main sections. The first, GETTING READY, offers an *Overview*, which states what children will be doing, and why, and provides a list of "What You'll Need." Specific numbers of Tangram pieces or entire sets are suggested on this list but can be adjusted as the needs of your specific situation dictate. Before the activity, Tangram pieces or sets can be counted out and placed in containers or self-sealing plastic bags for easy distribution. Blackline masters that are provided for your convenience at the back of the book are referenced on this materials list. Paper, pencils, scissors, tape, and materials for making charts, which may be necessary in some activities, are not.

Although overhead Tangram pieces and overhead Tangram recording paper are always listed in "What You'll Need" as optional, these materials are highly effective when you want children to see a demonstration using Tangrams. As you move the pieces on the screen, children can work with the same materials at their seats. Children can also use the overhead to present their work to other members of their group or to the class.

The second section, THE ACTIVITY, first presents a possible scenario for *Introducing* the children to the activity. The aim of this brief introduction is to help you give children the tools they will need to investigate independently. However, care has been taken to avoid undercutting the activity itself. Since these investigations are designed to enable children to increase their own mathematical power, the idea is to set the stage but not steal the show! The heart of the lesson, *On Their Own*, is found in a box at the top of the second page of each lesson. Here, rich problems stimulate many different problem-solving approaches and lead to a variety of solutions. These hands-on explorations have the potential for bringing children to new mathematical ideas and deepening their mathematical skills.

On Their Own is intended as a stand-alone activity for children to explore with a partner or in a small group. Be sure to make the needed directions clearly visible. You may want to write them on the chalkboard or on an overhead or present them either on reusable cards or paper. For children who may have difficulty reading the directions, you can read them aloud or make sure that each group includes at least one "reader".

The last part of this second section, *The Bigger Picture*, gives suggestions for how children can share their work and their thinking and make mathematical connections. Class charts and children's recorded work provide a springboard for discussion. Under "Thinking and Sharing," there are several prompts that you can use to promote discussion. Children will not be able to respond to these prompts with one-word answers. Instead, the prompts encourage children to describe what they notice, tell how they found their results, and give the reasoning behind their answers. Thus children learn to verify their own results rather than relying on the teacher to determine if an answer is "right" or "wrong." Though the class discussion might immediately follow the investigation, it is important not to cut the activity short by having a class discussion too soon.

The Bigger Picture often includes a suggestion for a "Writing" (or drawing) assignment. This is meant to help children process what they have just been doing. You might want to use these ideas as a focus for daily or weekly entries in a math journal that each child keeps.

1. I think I all depends on the role. If it has a lot of sides, use the small shapes. If it has only a few sides, use the big shapes.

2. We do not have a strategy!

3. The higher numbers are easier to make because it is easy to get shapes that way.

4. The most challenging part is get shapes with fewer sides and a lot of pieces.

From: *Shape Shifter*

The pieces that you use are the big triangle, and the two little triangles. First you take the big triangle and you place it like the head of an arrow pointing left. Then you take the two little triangles and put them on the long side of the big triangle. You put them together to form a medium triangle that looks like an head of an arrow pointing right.

* in the center.

From: *Tangram Recipe*

The Bigger Picture always ends with ideas for "Extending the Activity." Extensions take the essence of the main activity and either alter or extend its parameters. These activities are well used with a class that becomes deeply involved in the primary activity or for children who finish before the others. In any case, it is probably a good idea to expose the entire class to the possibility of, and the results from, such extensions.

The third and final section of the lesson is TEACHER TALK. Here, in *Where's the Mathematics?*, you can gain insight into the underlying mathematics of the activity and discover some of the strategies children are apt to use as they work. Solutions are also given—when such are necessary and/or helpful. Because *Where's the Mathematics?* provides a view of what may happen in the lesson as well as the underlying mathematical potential that may grow out of it, this may be the section that you want to read before presenting the activity to children.

USING THE ACTIVITIES

The Super Source® has been designed to fit into the variety of classroom environments in which it will be used. These range from a completely manipulative-based classroom to one in which manipulatives are just beginning to play a part. You may choose to use some activities in the Super Source in the way set forth in each lesson (introducing an activity to the whole class, then breaking the class up into groups that all work on the same task, and so forth). You will then be able to circulate among the groups as they work to observe and perhaps comment on each child's work. This approach requires a full classroom set of materials but allows you to concentrate on the variety of ways that children respond to a given activity.

Alternatively, you may wish to make two or three related activities available to different groups of children at the same time. You may even wish to use different manipulatives to explore the same mathematical concept. (Pattern Blocks and Geoboards, for example, can be used to teach some of the same geometric principles as Tangrams.) This approach does not require full classroom sets of a particular manipulative. It also permits greater adaptation of materials to individual children's needs and/or preferences.

If children are comfortable working independently, you might want to set up a "menu"— that is, set out a number of related activities from which children can choose. Children should be encouraged to write about their experiences with these independent activities.

However you choose to use the Super Source activities, it would be wise to allow time for several groups or the entire class to share their experiences. The dynamics of this type of interaction, where children share not only solutions and strategies but also feelings and intuitions, is the basis of continued mathematical growth. It allows children who are beginning to form a mathematical structure to clarify it and those who have mastered just isolated concepts to begin to see how these concepts might fit together.

Again, both the individual teaching style and combined learning styles of the children should dictate the specific method of utilizing the Super Source lessons. At first sight, some activities may appear too difficult for some of your children, and you may find yourself tempted to actually "teach" by modeling exactly how an activity can lead to a particular learning outcome. If you do this, you rob children of the chance to try the activity in whatever way they can. As long as children have a way to begin an investigation, give them time and opportunity to see it through. Instead of making assumptions about what children will or won't do, watch and listen. The excitement and challenge of the activity—as well as the chance to work cooperatively—may bring out abilities in children that will surprise you.

If you are convinced, however, that an activity does not suit your students, adjust it, by all means. You may want to change the language, either by simplifying it or by referring to specific vocabulary that you and your children already use and are comfortable with. On the other hand, if you suspect that an activity isn't challenging enough, you may want to read through the activity extensions for a variation that you can give children instead.

RECORDING

Although the direct process of working with Tangrams is a valuable one, it is afterward, when children look at, compare, share, and think about their constructions, that an activity yields its greatest rewards. However, because it is not always possible to leave Tangram constructions intact, children need an effective way to record their work and need to be encouraged to find ways to transfer their Tangram shapes. To this end, at the back of this book, Tangram paper is provided for reproduction, as are outlines of the Tangram pieces.

It is important that children use a method of recording that they feel comfortable with. Frustration in recording their shapes can leave children feeling that the actual activity was either too difficult or just not fun! Thus, recording methods that are appropriate for a specific class or for specific children might be suggested. For example, children might choose to trace each Tangram piece in their shape onto Tangram paper or onto plain paper, to cut out, color, and tape or paste down paper Tangram pieces, or they might use a Tangram template to reproduce the pieces that make up their shapes.

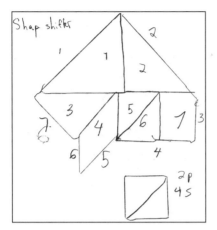

From: *Shape Shifter*

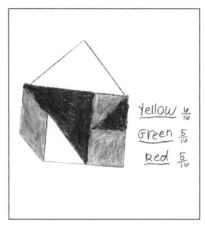

From: *Crazy Darts*

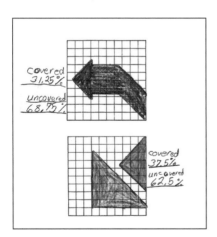

From: *Square Cover-Up*

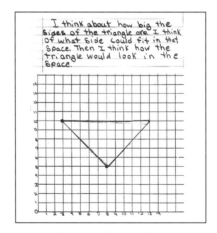

From: *Hit or Miss*

Another interesting way to "freeze" a Tangram shape is to create it using a software piece, such as *Journey with Tangrams* or *Shape Up!*, and then get a printout. Children can use a classroom or resource room computer if it is available or, where possible, extend the activity into a home assignment by utilizing their home computers. Since both children and adults enjoy Tangram puzzles, Tangrams, whether "in hand" or "on screen," can prove very helpful in making the home-school connection.

For many Tangram activities, recording involves copying the placement of the Tangram pieces. Yet, since there is a natural progression from thinking with manipulatives to a verbal description of what was done to a written record of it, as children work through the Tangram activities they should also be encouraged to record their thinking processes. Writing, drawing, and making charts and tables are also ways to record. By creating a table of data gathered in the course of their investigations, children are able to draw conclusions and look for patterns. When children write or draw, either in their group or later by themselves, they are clarifying their understanding of their recent mathematical experience.

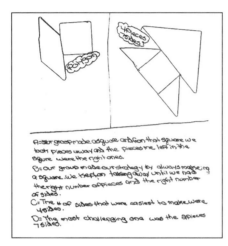

From: *Shape Shifter*

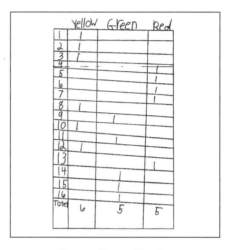

From: *Crazy Darts*

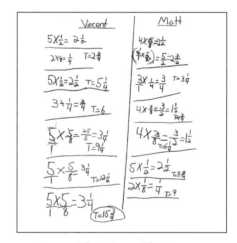

From: *What's Your Angle?*

From: *The More, The Better*

With a roomful of children busily engaged in their investigations, it is not easy for a teacher to keep track of how individual children are working. Having tangible material to gather and examine when the time is right will help you to keep in close touch with each child's learning.

Exploring Tangrams

The Tangram is a deceptively simple set of seven geometric shapes made up of five triangles (two small triangles, one medium triangle, and two large triangles), a square, and a parallelogram. When the pieces are arranged together they suggest an amazing variety of forms, embodying many numerical and geometric concepts. The Tangram pieces are widely used to solve puzzles which require the making of a specified shape using all seven pieces. ETA/Cuisenaire's seven-piece plastic Tangram set comes in in four colors—red, green, blue, and yellow. The three different-sized Tangram triangles are all similar, right isosceles triangles. Thus, the triangles all have angles of 45°, 45°, and 90°, and the corresponding sides of these triangles are in proportion.

Another interesting aspect of the Tangram set is that all of the Tangram pieces can be completely covered with small Tangram triangles.

small triangle   medium triangle   square   parallelogram   large triangle

Hence, it is easy to see that all the angles of the Tangram pieces are multiples of 45—that is, 45°, 90°, or 135°, and that the small Tangram triangle is the unit of measure that can be used to compare the areas of the Tangram pieces. Since the medium triangle, the square, and the parallelogram are each made up of two small Tangram triangles, they each have an area twice that of the small triangle. The large triangle is made up of four small Tangram triangles and thus has an area four times that of the small triangle and twice that of the other Tangram pieces.

Another special aspect of the pieces is that all seven fit together to form a square.

Some children can find the making of Tangram shapes to be very frustrating, especially if they are used to being able to "do" math by following rules and algorithms. For such children, you can reduce the level of frustration by providing some hints. For example, you can put down a first piece, or draw lines on an outline to show how pieces can be placed. However, it is important to find just the right level of challenge so that children can experience the pleasure of each Tangram investigation. Sometimes, placing some Tangram pieces incorrectly and then modeling an exploratory approach like the following may make children feel more comfortable: "I wonder if I could put this Tangram piece this way. I guess not, because then nothing else can fit here. So I'd better try another way...."

WORKING WITH TANGRAMS

Tangrams are a good tool for developing spatial reasoning and for exploring fractions and a variety of geometric concepts, including size, shape, congruence, similarity, area, perimeter, and the properties of polygons. Tangrams are especially suitable for children's independent work, since each child can be given a set for which he or she is responsible. However, since children vary greatly in their spatial abilities and language, some time should also be allowed for group work, and most children need ample time to experiment freely with Tangrams before they begin more serious investigations.

Young children will at first think of their Tangram shapes literally. With experience, they will see commonalities and begin to develop abstract language for aspects of patterns within their shapes. For example, children may at first make a square simply from two small triangles. Yet eventually they may develop an abstract mental image of a square divided by a diagonal into two triangles, which will enable them to build squares of other sizes from two triangles.

Tangrams can also provide a visual image essential for developing an understanding of fraction algorithms. Many children learn to do examples such as 1/2 = ?/8 or 1/4 + 1/8 + 1/16 = ? at a purely symbolic level so that if they forget the procedure, they are at a total loss. Children who have had many presymbolic experiences solving problems such as "Find how many small triangles fill the large triangles," or "How much of the full square is covered by a small, a medium, and a large triangle?" will have a solid intuitive foundation on which to build these basic skills and to fall back on if memory fails them.

Young children have an initial tendency to work with others, and to copy one another's work. Yet, even duplicating someone else's Tangram shape can expand a child's experience, develop the ability to recognize similarities and differences, and provide a context for developing language related to geometric ideas. Throughout their investigations, children should be encouraged to talk about their constructions in order to clarify and extend their thinking. For example, children will develop an intuitive feel for angles as they fit corners of Tangram pieces together, and they can be encouraged to think about why some will fit in a given space and others won't. Children can begin to develop a perception of symmetry as they take turns "mirroring" Tangram pieces across a line placed between them on a mat and can also begin to experience pride in their joint production.

Children of any age who haven't seen Tangrams before are likely to first explore shapes by building objects that look like objects—perhaps a butterfly, a rocket, a face, or a letter of the alphabet. Children with a richer geometric background are likely to impose interesting restrictions on their constructions, choosing to make, for example, a filled-in polygon, such as a square or hexagon, or a symmetric pattern.

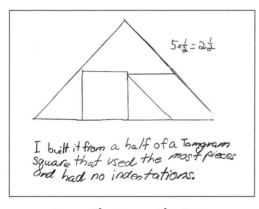

From: *The More, The Better*

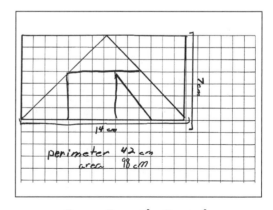

From: *Form the Formula*

ASSESSING CHILDREN'S UNDERSTANDING

The use of Tangrams provides a perfect opportunity for authentic assessment. Watching children work with the Tangram pieces gives you a visual sense of how they approach a mathematical problem. Their thinking can be "seen," in so far as that thinking is expressed through their positioning of the Tangram pieces, and when a class breaks up into small working groups, you are able to circulate, listen, and raise questions, all the while focusing on how individuals are thinking.

To ensure that children know not only how to do a certain operation but also how it relates to a model, assessment should include not only symbolic pencil-and-paper tasks such as "Find 1/2 + 1/8," but also performance tasks such as "Show why your answer is correct using Tangram pieces."

Having children describe their creations and share their strategies and thinking with the whole class gives you another opportunity for observational assessment. Furthermore, since spatial thinking plays an important role in children's intellectual development, include in your overall assessment some attention to spatial tasks.

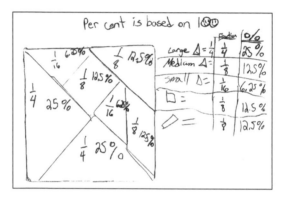

From: *Square Cover-Up*

Models of teachers assessing children's understanding can be found in ETA/Cuisenaire's series of videotapes listed below.

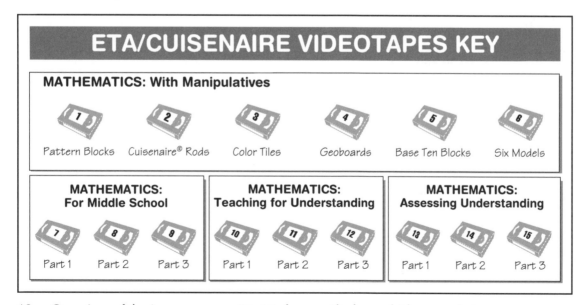

*See *Overview of the Lessons*, pages 16–17, for specific lesson/video correlation.

Connect
the Super Source®
to NCTM Standards.

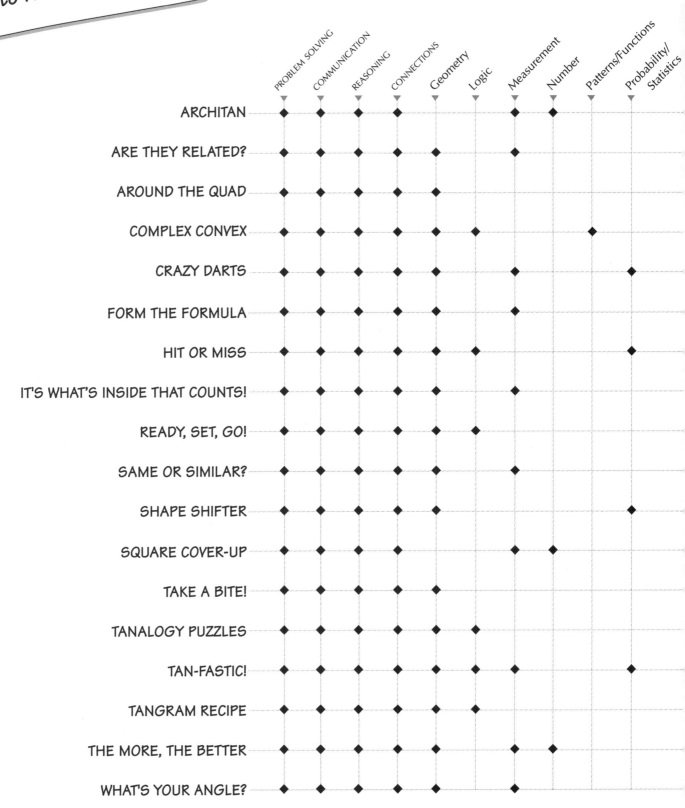

	PROBLEM SOLVING	COMMUNICATION	REASONING	CONNECTIONS	Geometry	Logic	Measurement	Number	Patterns/Functions	Probability/Statistics
ARCHITAN	◆	◆	◆	◆	◆		◆	◆		
ARE THEY RELATED?	◆	◆	◆	◆	◆		◆			
AROUND THE QUAD	◆	◆		◆						
COMPLEX CONVEX	◆	◆	◆	◆	◆	◆			◆	
CRAZY DARTS	◆	◆	◆	◆	◆		◆			◆
FORM THE FORMULA	◆	◆	◆	◆	◆		◆			
HIT OR MISS	◆	◆	◆	◆	◆	◆				◆
IT'S WHAT'S INSIDE THAT COUNTS!	◆	◆	◆	◆	◆		◆			
READY, SET, GO!	◆	◆	◆	◆	◆	◆				
SAME OR SIMILAR?	◆	◆	◆	◆	◆		◆			
SHAPE SHIFTER	◆	◆		◆	◆					◆
SQUARE COVER-UP	◆	◆	◆	◆	◆		◆	◆		
TAKE A BITE!	◆	◆	◆	◆	◆					
TANALOGY PUZZLES	◆	◆	◆	◆	◆	◆				
TAN-FASTIC!	◆	◆	◆	◆	◆	◆	◆			◆
TANGRAM RECIPE	◆	◆	◆	◆	◆	◆				
THE MORE, THE BETTER	◆	◆	◆	◆	◆		◆	◆		
WHAT'S YOUR ANGLE?	◆	◆	◆	◆	◆		◆			

Correlate *the Super Source®* to your curriculum.

	Angles	Area	Chance	Classifying	Comparing	Congruence	Estimation	Following directions	Fractional equivalence	Game strategies	Graphing	Percents	Perimeter	Polygons	Properties of geometric figures	Quadrilaterals	Ratio	Ratio and proportion	Similarity	Spatial visualization	Standard measurement	Symmetry	Transformational geometry
																		●	●				
		●											●										
																				●		●	●
				●	●									●									
		●	●														●						
		●																		●	●		
										●	●			●	●								
	●														●								
				●											●								
						●										●			●				
				●	●									●						●			
		●					●					●											
					●															●			●
					●										●								
		●		●			●			●					●								
								●						●						●			
		●	●	●					●					●						●			
	●													●	●								

Classroom-tested activities contained in these
Super Source Tangrams books focus on the
math strands in the charts below.

...the Super Source® Tangrams, Grades K-2

Geometry	Logic	Measurement
Number	**Patterns/Functions**	**Probability/Statistics**

...the Super Source® Tangrams, Grades 3-4

Geometry	Logic	Measurement
Number	**Patterns/Functions**	**Probability/Statistics**

More SUPER SOURCE®
at a glance:
ADDITIONAL MANIPULATIVES
for Grades 5–6

Classroom-tested activities contained in these *Super Source* books focus on the math strands as indicated in these charts.

...the Super Source® Snap™ Cubes, Grades 5–6

Geometry	Logic	Measurement
Number	Patterns/Functions	Probability/Statistics

...the Super Source® Color Tiles, Grades 5–6

Geometry	Logic	Measurement
Number	Patterns/Functions	Probability/Statistics

...the Super Source® Cuisenaire® Rods, Grades 5–6

Geometry	Logic	Measurement
Number	Patterns/Functions	Probability/Statistics

...the Super Source® Geoboards, Grades 5–6

Geometry	Logic	Measurement
Number	Patterns/Functions	Probability/Statistics

...the Super Source® Base Ten Blocks, Grades 5–6

Geometry	Logic	Measurement
Number	Patterns/Functions	Probability/Statistics

...the Super Source® Pattern Blocks, Grades 5–6

Geometry	Logic	Measurement
Number	Patterns/Functions	Probability/Statistics

Overview of the Lessons

Tangrams, Grades 5-6

 See video key, page 11.

ARCHITAN

Getting Ready

What You'll Need

Tangrams, 1 set per child

Tangram paper, several sheets per child, page 90

Scissors, 1 per child

Metric ruler, 1 per child

Protractor, 1 per child

Overhead Tangrams and/or Tangram paper transparency (optional)

Overview

Children make a set of Tangram pieces with sides that are three times longer than the those in the plastic Tangram set. In this activity, children have the opportunity to:

◆ apply the concept of similarity to pairs of polygons

◆ use ratio and proportion in measuring and enlarging polygons

The Activity

Children may use a metric ruler and a protractor to make the larger shape, or they may use the small Tangram triangle itself to measure sides and angles.

Introducing

◆ Display a small Tangram triangle. Ask children to work in pairs using any strategy they like to draw a triangle that has the same shape as this one but with sides that are twice as long.

◆ Compare the triangles and discuss the methods that were used to make the larger triangle similar to the original one.

◆ Point out the proportional relationships between the triangles noting that in similar triangles, sides must be in proportion, and corresponding angles must be congruent. If necessary, review the notation for representing a scale of the ratio; in this case:

1 to 2 or 1:2

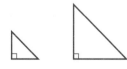

On Their Own

> **Can you create a set of Tangram pieces whose sides are 3 times as long as the sides of the original piece?**
>
> - Be an architect and use your Tangram set as a blueprint to construct a larger set of paper Tangram pieces. Make the ratio of each side of a plastic Tangram piece to the corresponding side in the larger set 1 to 3.
>
> - Copy the new set of pieces onto Tangram paper.
>
> - Cut out your pieces.
>
> - Be ready to tell how you know that each piece is similar to, or is an enlargement of, the corresponding Tangram piece.

The Bigger Picture

Thinking and Sharing

Use prompts like these to promote class discussion:

- What strategies did you use to make enlargements of the pieces? Did you use the same strategies for all the pieces? If not, why?

- What is the same about a piece and its enlargement? What's different?

- Which piece was the easiest to enlarge? Which was the hardest?

- Did you have to measure every side of every piece before enlarging it? Why or why not?

- What pieces from the Tangram set were already similar? How do you know?

Writing

Have children describe how they could enlarge this shape made from Tangram pieces.

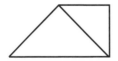

Extending the Activity

Have children make another set of Tangrams, this time using the enlargement of the medium triangle they made in this activity as the smallest piece.

Where's the Mathematics?

As children work through this activity, they see what happens to lengths and angles when polygons are enlarged. Using problem solving and measuring skills, children apply scale ratios in a concrete situation. They see how change in scale affects the measurement of the sides, angles, and area of polygons.

Children may approach the problem of making their enlargements in a variety of ways. Some children may make a large square with sides three times longer than a square built from one set of Tangram pieces. These children may then fold or draw lines within the square to make the larger Tangram pieces.

Size of Square Built From
Actual Tangram Pieces

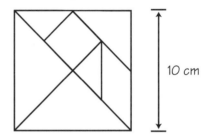

10 cm

Other children may approach the task by measuring sides and angles and enlarging pieces one at a time. For example:

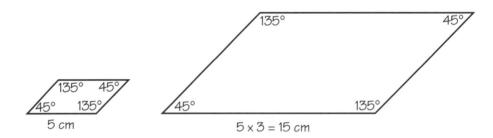

135°   45°
45°   135°
5 cm

135°   45°

45°   135°
5 x 3 = 15 cm

Children may have used a protractor to measure the angles or may have measured angles by using triangles.

 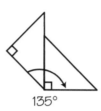

As children see the need to measure lines and angles, they may substitute the use of the small Tangram triangle for the ruler. These children may note that all of the Tangram sides can be measured with the sides of the small triangle.

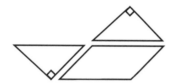

Children who have had experience measuring area with a small Tangram triangle may use this knowledge to enlarge the Tangram set. Once children have made the small triangle in the larger scale, they can make copies of that triangle and then use them to build the remaining Tangram pieces.

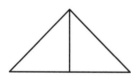

ARE THEY RELATED?

Getting Ready

What You'll Need

Tangrams, 1 set per pair

Metric ruler, 1 per pair

1-Centimeter grid paper, page 91,
1 sheet per pair (optional)

Calculator, 1 per child (optional)

Overhead Tangram pieces and/or
Tangram paper transparency (optional)

Overview

Using all seven Tangram pieces, children try to make a shape with the
least perimeter. In this activity, children have the opportunity to:

♦ develop basic measurement skills and concepts to find area
and perimeter

♦ explore the relationship between area and perimeter

The Activity

*Children may suggest various ways to
find the areas and perimeters. Some
children may measure or calculate,
while others will find innovative
methods.*

Introducing

♦ Display the square Tangram piece and ask children how they would
find the *area* of the square, or amount of space the square covers.
Have them demonstrate their methods.

♦ Now ask children how they would find the *perimeter* of the square,
or distance around it, and have them
demonstrate their methods.

♦ Display the shape shown here. Ask children
how they could find its area and perimeter.

On Their Own

How can you use all 7 Tangram pieces to make a shape with the least possible perimeter?

- Work with a partner to use all 7 Tangram pieces to make a shape.

- Slide your shape onto a piece of paper. Trace around the outside of the shape.

- Find the area of your shape, or amount of space it covers. Write the area in the center of the tracing.

- Find the perimeter of your shape, or distance around it. Write the perimeter outside the tracing.

- Discuss possible ways to rearrange the Tangram pieces in order to make a shape with a lesser perimeter.

- Work together to make a shape with the least perimeter possible. Trace that shape and record its perimeter.

The Bigger Picture

Thinking and Sharing

Ask pairs to post the shapes they made.

Use prompts such as these to promote class discussion:

- ◆ What do you notice about the posted shapes?

- ◆ What methods did you use to find the area of Tangram shapes?

- ◆ What methods did you use to find the perimeter of Tangram shapes?

- ◆ How did you rearrange pieces in order to reduce the perimeter of your shape?

- ◆ Does rearranging the Tangram pieces in a shape change the area? the perimeter? Explain.

- ◆ How are the area and perimeter of a shape related?

Drawing and Writing

Tell children to imagine they are told the area of a polygon. Ask them if they can draw any conclusions about the perimeter of that polygon. Have them explain their thinking and include drawings with their work.

Teacher Talk

Where's the Mathematics?

As children find area and perimeter in this activity, they have the opportunity to use problem-solving strategies to find shortcuts to simplify the task. Children may see many ways in which the Tangram pieces are related. For example, children may observe that there are only four different side lengths in the Tangram set.

| large triangle | medium triangle | parallelogram | square | small triangle |

Children may realize that the area of all of the Tangram pieces can be found by using the area of the Tangram square as a measuring unit. Thus, the area of the small triangle is half the area of the square. The areas of each of the parallelogram and medium triangle are equal to that of the square since, like the square, each can be covered by two small Tangram triangles. The area of the large triangle is double that of the square, since it can be covered by two medium triangles.

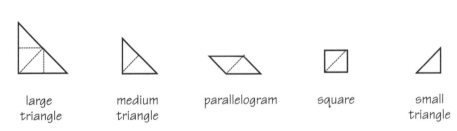

| large triangle | medium triangle | parallelogram | square | small triangle |

As children make, trace, and measure shapes, they may conclude that since the same pieces are used in each shape, any arrangement of them will have the same area. When comparing shapes made from all seven Tangram pieces, children may note that shapes with fewer sides usually have a shorter perimeters. They may also observe that convex shapes usually have shorter perimeters than concave shapes or that the more compact shapes usually have shorter perimeters than the less compact ones.

Extending the Activity

Challenge children to use one set of Tangrams to build a shape with the greatest possible perimeter.

These shapes may be similar to those made by your class, and are arranged in order from greatest to least perimeter.

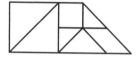 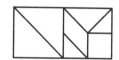

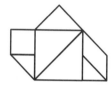 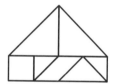

Children may find innovative ways to find the perimeter of each shape. For example, they may run a string around the outline of the shape and then measure the length of the string with a metric ruler. Some children might simply use one side of a Tangram piece to measure around the edge of the shape, and then multiply the length of that side by the number of times they used it.

If children choose to use grid paper to find area, their numbers may not be exact. These children may want to confirm their findings using area formulas. Even if two groups disagree on measurements, they should still reach the same conclusions about the relationship between area and perimeter.

AROUND THE QUAD

- **Transformational geometry**
- **Symmetry**
- **Spatial visualization**

Getting Ready

What You'll Need

Tangrams, 2 sets per group of 4

Rulers, 1 per group

Mirrors, 1 per group (optional)

Quadrant paper, 1 sheet per group, page 92

Overhead Tangram pieces and/or 1-Centimeter grid paper transparency (optional)

Overview

Children create designs with Tangram pieces using reflective symmetry. In this activity, children have the opportunity to:

- make predictions about the transformation of shapes
- analyze the properties of polygons

The Activity

Introducing

- Draw intersecting perpendicular lines, or axis lines, on the chalkboard and tell children that you have created four regions called quadrants. Have children fold a piece of paper horizontally and vertically, then unfold it and trace along the fold lines to divide their paper into the fourths or quadrants.

- Place a large Tangram triangle on the board in the upper right quadrant so that it is positioned as shown. Trace around it.

- Now ask children to place a large Tangram triangle on their paper in the same position in that quadrant and to trace around it.

- Tell children to pretend that the vertical and horizontal axis lines are mirrors, and ask them to show on their paper how the triangle would look reflected in each of the mirrors.

- Then at the board flip, or reflect, the triangle across each axis, trace it in each position, and have children compare their work with yours.

- Discuss with children the possible triangle reflections that would complete the design in the last quadrant.

On Their Own

Can you make a Tangram shape using line symmetry?

- Sit in a circle with the other members of your group. Place a piece of quadrant paper that looks like this in the center of the circle. Pretend that the heavy intersecting lines, or axis lines, are mirrors. As you work together, each person in your group will be responsible for 1 of the sections, or quadrants.

- Decide who will be the first Design Starter. The Design Starter places any Tangram piece in his or her quadrant, traces it, colors it, and passes the design to the group member to the left.

- That group member flips, or reflects, the Tangram piece across a mirror into his or her quadrant, traces it, colors it, and passes it to the left. This continues until the piece appears in all 4 quadrants.

- Now another group member becomes the Design Starter, adding a piece to the design. The process continues until everyone has had a chance to be the Design Starter.

The Bigger Picture

Thinking and Sharing

Post the designs made by the groups. Discuss any similarities and differences.

Use prompts like these to promote class discussion:

- Which Tangram pieces were easiest to flip, or reflect, and place correctly? Which were hardest?

- How did you use the axis lines to help you reflect and place pieces?

- How do you know when a piece is placed correctly?

- When you place and reflect a square, is the reflection different from the original square? Explain.

- How do you know your entire design shows reflective, or line, symmetry?

- How would your design be different if it had been reflected over only one axis, or had just one line of symmetry?

- Could you make a design with more than two axis lines? How would it look different from the design your group made?

Writing

Have children explain to a friend how to divide a piece of unlined paper into quadrants.

Extending the Activity

1. Have a child be the Shape Designer who builds a design in one section of a piece of quadrant paper using four to seven Tangram pieces. Then

Teacher Talk

Where's the Mathematics?

As children flip and trace Tangram pieces, they gain a concrete experience with reflective symmetry. The visual and spatial skills children may acquire are important in building an understanding of relationships and constructions of geometric figures which will be useful for solving more complex geometric problems.

Children may observe that it is easier to flip a Tangram piece accurately when the piece is aligned with one of the axis lines. Children may also note that the orientation of the Tangram triangle piece and the square may change when they are reflected.

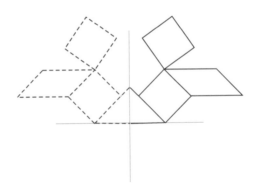

During the *On Their Own* activity, children may begin to anticipate how to place the Tangram piece in their quadrant and trace the piece immediately, not waiting for the movement to proceed clockwise around the quadrants. Some children may enjoy challenging the group by coming up with a difficult placement.

After flipping and tracing a piece, children may use different strategies to check whether or not the transformation has been done properly. They may use mirrors to check their work, turn the paper over, or rotate the paper to see if the design looks the same. Some children may fold the paper along axis lines to see if the Tangram pieces line up.

ask the group members to use a separate piece of paper, assign themselves different quadrants, and build the design as it should look in their quadrant. After all group members trace and color their designs, have them cut them out and fit them together to make the whole design. Then ask the group to check their designs and make corrections if necessary.

2. Have children repeat the activity adding two "diagonal" axis lines so that the quadrant paper is divided into eight equal sections.

As children work with Tangram pieces, they may notice that the Tangram triangles have one line of symmetry, the square has four lines of symmetry, and the parallelogram has none. To test this idea, children may place a Tangram piece across an axis line so that one-half of the piece lies on each side of the line. If the piece has reflective symmetry, the shape on one side of the line should be the mirror image of the shape on the other side.

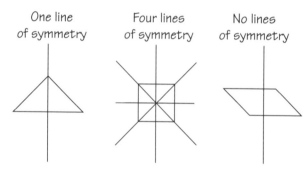

One line of symmetry   Four lines of symmetry   No lines of symmetry

The following designs may be similar to those your class will make.

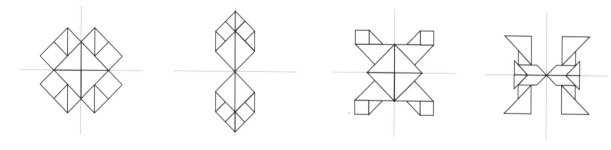

As children think about decreasing or increasing the number of axis lines, they may give examples of familiar objects that demonstrate line symmetry. For example, the human face and body have one line of symmetry, while a snowflake is formed along three axis lines. You may find that some children speculate that the greater the number of axis lines, the more the design or object approximates a circular shape.

COMPLEX CONVEX

- Comparing
- Classifying
- Polygons

Getting Ready

What You'll Need

Tangrams, 1 set per child

8"-10" piece of string, 1 per child

Overhead Tangram pieces (optional)

Overview

Children search for all the convex polygons that can be made using a seven-piece Tangram set. In this activity, children have the opportunity to:

◆ apply spatial reasoning

◆ classify and compare polygons

◆ develop strategies to determine whether a polygon is concave or convex

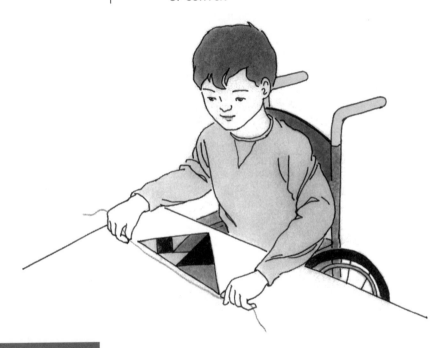

The Activity

If children need hints to help them find solutions, use the overhead projector to display some prepared silhouettes of concave and convex polygons.

Introducing

- Display this concave polygon made with Tangram pieces, and have children copy it. Demonstrate how to connect each pair of consecutive corners with a string to decide if the polygon is *concave*, or dented inward. If the string remains outside the polygon, the polygon is concave.

Concave (Indent)

String

- Have children add one more Tangram piece to change the concave polygon into one that is *convex*, with no indents. Point out that no matter which two corners of the convex polygon the string connects, it lies either along a side or within the polygon.

Convex (No indent)

String

©ETA/Cuisenaire®

On Their Own

How many different convex polygons can you build?

- Using 1 set of 7 Tangram pieces, design as many polygons as you can that are convex (that have no indents).

- Check with a string to be sure that your polygons are convex. If you connect any 2 corners of a polygon and the string stays outside the polygon, then the polygon is *concave*. But if the string goes inside the polygon or along one of its sides, then the polygon is convex.

Concave (Indent)

Convex (No indent)

- Trace around each piece to record your convex polygons. Then cut them out.

- Compare the cut-out polygons to make sure they are all different.

The Bigger Picture

Thinking and Sharing

After children have designed as many different polygons as they can, have them order them by the number of sides. Ask children for the least and greatest number of sides they found. Write this range of numbers on the board. Then invite children to post different examples for each number.

Children may find it helpful to stack their polygons over one another to check for congruent polygons.

Use prompts like these to promote class discussion:

- Do you think we found all the possible convex polygons? Why or why not?

- What strategies did you use to design convex polygons?

- What methods did you use to check that a new solution was different from one already found?

- Do you think there might be a solution with more than six sides? Why or why not?

- Do you think are more, fewer, or the same number of concave polygons as convex polygons that can be made with a set of Tangram pieces? Explain.

Drawing

Have children find three objects in the room that have a surface that is a convex polygon. Ask them to draw the objects and then to label the part of the illustration that is convex.

Extending the Activity

Challenge children repeat the activity, this time creating polygons from two sets of Tangrams.

Teacher Talk

Where's the Mathematics?

As they design convex polygons, children explore geometric relationships among Tangram pieces. Using a string to test whether polygons are concave or convex gives children opportunities to validate their spatial intuition.

When exploring solutions for *Complex Convex*, some children may use trial and error to design polygons. Others may find one solution, like the square or rectangle shown below, and experiment systematically by moving a few pieces to find another solution.

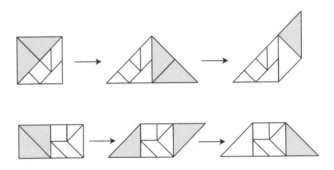

To test their polygons, some children will rely solely on the string test. Other children may observe that all the interior angles in a convex shape are less than 180° and use this fact to test the shapes they build. Still other children may rely on spatial visualization, looking to see if any corners of the shape are "pushed or caved in."

Children may be surprised to find that there is a limited number of ways to form convex polygons with seven Tangram pieces. They may also realize that often a different arrangement of pieces may produce the same polygon.

If transformations and Tangram-piece arrangements are excluded, children may find 13 solutions as follows.

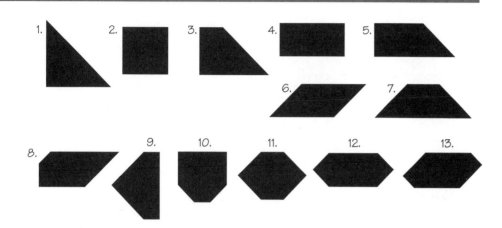

As they examine the 13 convex polygons, children may notice that there are more polygons with an even number of sides than an odd number of sides.

Of the 13 polygons, one is a triangle, six are quadrilaterals, two are pentagons, and four are hexagons. Here are possible arrangements of Tangram pieces for the 13 convex polygons.

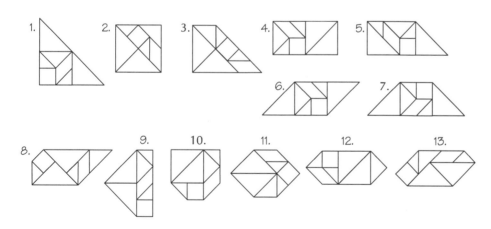

Children may observe that it is easier to make concave polygons than convex ones. Some children may suggest trying to find the number of concave polygons possible with seven Tangrams. If children choose to try this experiment, they may quickly discover that this is a big job. There are, in fact, over 1,000 possible concave polygons.

CRAZY DARTS

- Ratio
- Area
- Chance

Getting Ready

What You'll Need

Tangrams, 1 set per child

Crayons or markers

Small object such as a coin, counter, bean, or seed, 1 per child

Overhead Tangram pieces (optional)

Overview

Children design and color a dartboard made from Tangram pieces and then find the probability of an object landing on each color. In this activity, children have the opportunity to:

- ◆ create and compare a variety of polygons
- ◆ determine the ratio of one area to another

The Activity

Some children may find it helpful to use different colored Tangram sets in order to determine placement of colors.

Introducing

- ◆ Ask children if they have ever played a game in which they had to hit a target to earn points. Discuss their answers.

- ◆ Then trace the following Tangram pieces on the board and tell children that you have made a polygon, and that you would like to color it with the fewest colors possible to make a Tangram dartboard.

- ◆ First explain that the same color pieces may touch at a corner or point but not along a side. Have children suggest possible color schemes for the Tangram dartboard.

- ◆ Using one of the suggested color schemes, trace and color a copy of the Tangram dartboard and drop a small object, "the dart," on it from a distance of about one foot.

- ◆ Explain to children that this is a method that can be used to find how often the object falls into each "color" section.

On Their Own

Can you find the probability of a "dart" hitting each of the colors on a dartboard?

- Work with a partner, and make a polygon using a set of 7 Tangram pieces.

- Slide your polygon onto a sheet of paper. Trace it. Include the outline of each Tangram piece. This is your Tangram dartboard.

- Color the Tangram dartboard using as few colors as possible. Make sure that the same color pieces touch only at the corners.

- Conduct a probability experiment: Drop a "dart," which can be any small object, onto the Tangram dartboard. Keep a record of the color of the piece on which the dart lands. Repeat this process until you have made 16 tries.

- Based on the results of your experiment, write the probability of landing on each color as a ratio this way:

$$\frac{\text{number of times the object landed on the color}}{\text{total number of tries}}$$

The Bigger Picture

Thinking and Sharing

Invite children to post their dartboards and the results of their probability experiments.

Use prompts like these to promote class discussion:

- What do you notice about the posted dartboards?

- How did you decide what shape dartboard to build and how to color it?

- Did your probability experiment turn out as you thought it would? Explain.

- Would you agree with someone who said that no matter how the dartboards are colored, there is an equal chance of hitting each color? How would you convince that person of your point of view?

- If you repeat the probability experiment using the same Tangram dartboard, do you think the results will be the same? Explain.

- If you rearrange the pieces on your dartboard without changing the color of any piece, would the probabilities change? Explain.

- If you change the colors on your dartboard, but keep the same arrangement of pieces, would the probabilities change? Explain.

Extending the Activity

1. Have children repeat the activity using two sets of Tangrams and conducting the probability experiment with 32 trials.

2. Challenge children to make a dartboard using one set of Tangrams, this time coloring the board so that there is an equal chance of hitting any color.

Where's the Mathematics?

In this activity, children are given opportunities to investigate geometric and numerical relationships. As they create the shape and color arrangement of their Tangram dartboards, children can gain a greater understanding of the properties of polygons. As they compute probabilities, children can strengthen their understanding of the concepts of area, ratios, fractions, percents, and chance.

Children can create many different polygons using all seven Tangram pieces. Here are some examples of convex polygons:

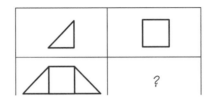

Here are some examples of concave polygons:

Children may discover that the same dartboard can be colored in more than one way. All boards can be colored with either two or three colors, and as children search for the best way to color their dartboard, they may realize that by moving pieces, they can reduce the number of colors.

Some children may talk about probability informally using statements such as "You have a good chance of hitting the red," or "There's so much blue, there is no way you can land on red."

Other children may express their understanding of probability using ratios, fractions, or percents. For example, "Since half the shape is red, you have a 50% chance of hitting red," or "There's twice as much green as blue so you have twice as much chance to land on green as on blue."

Some children may base their observations about probability on the area of each color. For example, any polygon made from one set of Tangram pieces will have an area equal to 16 small Tangram triangles.

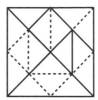

total area = 16 small triangle units

In the polygon below it would take three small triangles to cover the red pieces, five to cover all the blue, and eight to cover all the green. Thus, the ratios of the areas of each section of color to the whole area are 3:16 for red, 5:16 for blue, and 8:16 (or 1:2) for green. Children may also set up these ratios as fractions: ³⁄₁₆ for red, ⁵⁄₁₆ for blue, and ⁸⁄₁₆ or ½ for green.

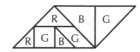

Some children may observe that rearranging the pieces that make up their Tangram dartboard does not change the area and thus the probabilities do not change.

White = 5/16 or 5:16
Gray = 11/16 or 11:16

Some children may note that changing the colors in the same arrangement of Tangram pieces does not change the probabilities either.

White = 7/16 or 7:16
Black = 5/16 or 5:16
Gray = 4/16 (or 1/4) or 4:16

White = 6/16 (or 3/8) or 6:16
Black = 4/16 (or 1/4) or 4:16
Gray = 6/16 (or 3/8) or 6:16

FORM THE FORMULA

- Area
- Spatial visualization
- Standard measurement

Getting Ready

What You'll Need

Tangrams, 1 set per child

1-Centimeter grid paper, 2 sheets per child, page 91

Metric ruler, 1 per child

Overhead Tangram pieces and/or 1-Centimeter grid paper transparency

Overview

Children use Tangram pieces to build rectangles and parallelograms in order to derive their area formulas. In this activity, children have the opportunity to:

- see how area is conserved when the same Tangram pieces are used to form different shapes
- improve their measurement skills using metric units
- observe patterns in the relationship between the dimensions of a quadrilateral and its area

The Activity

Introducing

- Display a rectangle made from a Tangram square and two small triangles.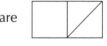

- Have children copy the rectangle with their Tangram pieces and trace it on 1-cm grid paper. Then have children measure the base and height with their metric rulers.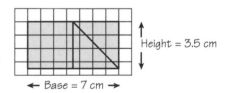

  Height = 3.5 cm
  ← Base = 7 cm →

- Demonstrate how the rectangle can be changed to a parallelogram by moving one piece. Have children copy the shape and trace it on grid paper.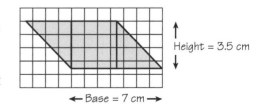

  Height = 3.5 cm
  ← Base = 7 cm →

- Discuss how the base and height of the parallelogram compare to those of the rectangle.

On Their Own

> ### Can you figure out formulas for finding the area of rectangles and parallelograms?
>
> - Sit in a circle with the other members of your group. Each of you makes a different rectangle using 4 to 7 Tangram pieces. Work together to make sure that the rectangles are different.
>
> - Position your rectangle on 1-centimeter grid paper and trace each piece. Measure its base and height. Then count the square centimeters your rectangle covers to find its area. You might have to estimate the partial squares.
>
> - Record the measurements. Here's an example using 3 Tangram pieces:
>
> - Now pass your rectangle to the person on your left.
>
>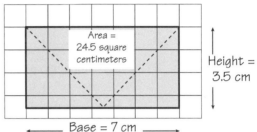
>
> - Change your *new* rectangle into a non-rectangular parallelogram using the same Tangram pieces. Trace the outline onto grid paper and find and record the base, the height, and the area. Remember, you may have to estimate some measurements.
>
> - Compare the measurements for the set of related shapes.
>
> - Work together to find patterns in your data that may help you to predict the areas of rectangles and parallelograms.

The Bigger Picture

Thinking and Sharing

Create a class chart by asking volunteers to post the rectangles in one column, arranged by area from least to greatest. Include only one sample for each different area measurement. Make a second column in which to have volunteers post the related non-rectangular parallelograms.

Use prompts such as these to promote class discussion:

- What do you notice as you look at each column on the chart? each row?

- Was it possible to change every one of your rectangles into parallelograms? Explain.

- How did you find the base and the height of each shape?

- How did you find the area of each shape?

- When you changed a rectangle into a parallelogram using the same Tangram pieces, what happened to the measurement of the base? the height? the area?

- As you look at the chart, what patterns do you notice?

- How can the patterns you found help you to find the areas of these shapes?

Writing

Have children explain how they were able to change a rectangle into a non-rectangular parallelogram using the same Tangram pieces.

When working with rectangles, children may choose to use the terms length *and* width *instead of* base *and* height.

Where's the Mathematics?

Some children may have memorized area formulas for shapes but not have a clear understanding of why the formulas work. As they measure the base and height of shapes and look for patterns, they see the relationship between dimensions and area. As they use grid paper to measure area, children also may gain a concrete understanding of the meaning of area and develop strategies for measuring it.

Depending on how children line up the sides of their shapes with the grid lines, they may have difficulty finding the area in square centimeters accurately and may need to double check their work by making a second tracing in a new position and recounting the square centimeters. Children may need to be assured that in this activity, when finding the base, the height, and especially the area, it is acceptable to estimate their answers. Here are some of the rectangles children may form.

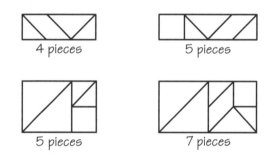

| 4 pieces | 5 pieces |
| 5 pieces | 7 pieces |

After measuring the base, height, and area of their rectangles, some children may immediately recognize that the area is equal to the base times the height. Other children may focus on finding a relationship between the base and the height. These children may notice that for some shapes made from Tangram pieces the base is equal to twice the height.

Some children may be surprised that the area of their non-rectangular parallelogram is not equal to the product of the length of two consecutive sides. Children may need to review the concept of *height* as the perpendicular distance between the bases.

Extending the Activity

Ask children to repeat the activity using three or more pieces from two Tangram sets. Have them order their solutions by area from least to greatest.

As children work to transform shapes, some may immediately grasp that moving the Tangram pieces will not change the area. If they have successfully derived the area formula for the rectangle, they may be able to build on their experience to create a formula for finding the area of a non-rectangular parallelogram.

One possible transformation is shown below:

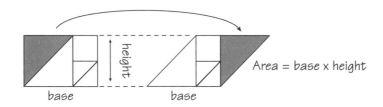

All four of the rectangles possible in the activity can be changed into non-rectangular parallelograms by moving one tangram piece, as shown below:

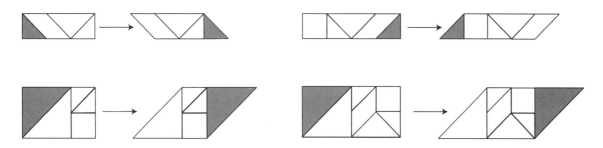

If children have had previous experience measuring the area of Tangram shapes using small Tangram triangles, they may already understand the concept of conservation of area. These children may see that the area of the quadrilateral is equal to the sum of the areas of each of the pieces in the shape, regardless of how and where the pieces are placed.

Some children may have difficulty explaining why multiplying the base by the height allows them to find the area of a non-rectangular parallelogram. In addition to tracing shapes and counting squares on grid paper, paper cutting and folding may help children see how rectangles and non-rectangular parallelograms are related. Understanding this relationship can be a springboard for investigations about the areas of triangles and trapezoids as well as the areas of irregular polygons.

HIT OR MISS

- Graphing
- Properties of polygons
- Game strategies

Getting Ready

What You'll Need

Tangrams, 1 set per pair

1-Centimeter grid paper, several sheets per child, page 91

Overhead Tangram pieces and 1-Centimeter grid paper transparency (optional)

Overview

In this game for two players, children use a coordinate grid to guess the location of a hidden Tangram piece. In this activity, children have the opportunity to:

- ◆ visualize spatial relationships of polygons
- ◆ explore coordinate graphing
- ◆ practice using logic

The Activity

Children may want to use a marker or colored pencil to darken the axis lines of the grid.

Introducing

- ◆ Using 1-centimeter grid paper, show children how to make a coordinate system by numbering each line from 0 to 14 as shown.

- ◆ Ask children to start at 0 and locate a point by moving 5 lines to the right and 4 lines up. Have them mark that point and identify it with the ordered pair (5,4), as shown.

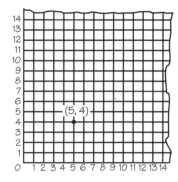

- ◆ Now have them position the medium Tangram triangle so that one of the corners touches point (5,4) and each of the other two corners touches a point where two of the lines cross on the grid.

- ◆ Discuss the various possible triangle positions.

- ◆ Ask children to reposition the triangle so that (5,4) is first on a side of the triangle, then inside the triangle, and finally outside the triangle. Discuss some of the possibilities for the new triangle positions.

On Their Own

Play Hit or Miss!

Here are the rules:

1. This is a game for 2 players. The object is to locate the 3 corners of a partner's hidden triangle.

2. Both players need a large Tangram triangle and a piece of 1-centimeter grid paper. The players should have a barrier between them so they cannot see each other's workspace.

Point of intersection

3. Players each "hide" a large Tangram triangle somewhere on their grids, by placing it so that each corner touches a point of intersection where 2 grid lines cross.

4. Players take turns trying to guess the ordered pairs that mark the corner points of the hidden triangles. For each ordered pair that a player guesses, the other player responds in 1 of these ways:

   Corner Hit—if the corner of the triangle touches the point.
   Side Hit—if the side of the triangle touches the point.
   Inside Hit—if the triangle covers up the point.
   Outside Miss—if the point is outside the triangle.

5. Players keep track of their hits and misses. The player who locates each corner of the other player's triangle wins.

• Play several games of *Hit or Miss*.

• Be ready to talk about your strategies.

The Bigger Picture

Thinking and Sharing

Invite children to talk about their games and describe some of the thinking they did.
Use prompts like these to promote class discussion:

♦ When you first played the game, how did you decide where to hide your triangle?

♦ How did you keep track of your hits and misses? Was this way helpful?

♦ Which responses from your partner were most helpful? Which were least helpful?

♦ When you scored a "corner hit," how did you use that information to help you make your next guess?

♦ What advice would you give to someone who was about to play this game for the first time?

♦ If you were to play this game again, what would you do differently? Why?

Drawing and Writing

Have children imagine that they are playing *Hit or Miss* and that they get corner hits for these ordered pairs: (3,10) and (8,5). Ask them to draw the large Tangram triangle on the grid and write a paragraph explaining how they know their triangle is correct.

Teacher Talk

Where's the Mathematics?

When playing *Hit or Miss*, children experiment with game strategies and logic while learning about coordinate graphs. As children analyze how ordered pairs can be used to define a triangle, they improve their spatial visualization skills.

During the activity, children may develop a greater understanding of geometric language, using words such as *sides, vertex, area, intersection, plotting, axis, coordinates,* and *ordered pairs*.

When playing the game, players may decide to trace their hidden shapes to make room on the grid to plot their opponents' guesses. They may also choose to place a large Tangram triangle on the grid where they are recording their guesses to help them visualize how the hidden triangle could be positioned.

Children may create their own strategies for recording guesses. They may use letters to mark the points: *C* for Corner Hit, *S* for Side Hit, *I* for Inside Hit, and *M* for Miss. Other children may record guesses by writing ordered pairs in a T-table as shown below.

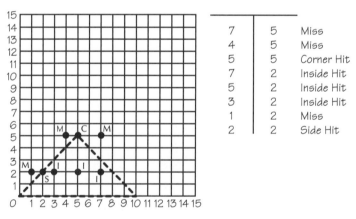

Initially, children may guess ordered pairs at random. Some may choose opposite areas on the grid until there is a hit. As play progresses, they may begin to use strategic thinking. For example, after scoring an Inside Hit, a player may try to locate a side and then work toward a corner to establish the boundaries of the triangle.

Children may decide that some kinds of Hits are more helpful than others. They may note that a Corner Hit helps them begin to see the orientation of the triangle. Since the short side of the large triangle is seven centimeters in length, children may count seven spaces from a Corner Hit to make their next guess. Other children may prefer to work from space to space along a side of the triangle.

Extending the Activity

1. Have children play the game *Hit or Miss* again using two Tangram pieces on their grids at the same time.

2. Have children repeat the game *Hit or Miss*, but this time allow the responding partner to give only the messages "Hit" or "Miss."

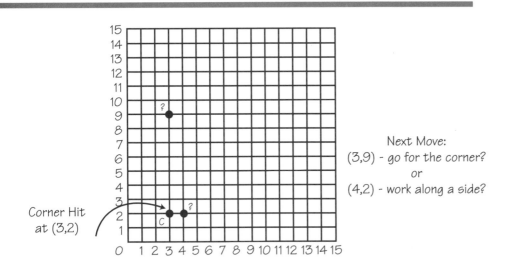

Corner Hit at (3,2)

Next Move:
(3,9) - go for the corner?
or
(4,2) - work along a side?

Children may decide that the position of the triangle is easier to plot when the short sides are oriented horizontally and vertically on the grid. Children may find the position more difficult to discover when the hypotenuse is horizontal or vertical.

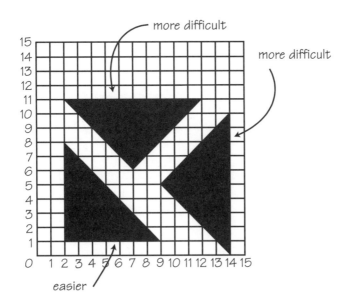

more difficult

more difficult

easier

Playing *Hit or Miss* not only develops an understanding of the coordinate system and the use of ordered pairs for plotting points on a graph but it also prepares children to understand how ordered pairs can be used to graph a line, determine the slope of a line, and find the distance between two points on a line.

IT'S WHAT'S INSIDE THAT COUNTS!

* Properties of geometric figures
* Angles

Getting Ready

What You'll Need

Tangrams, 1 set per pair

Protractor, 1 per pair

Calculator, 1 per pair (optional)

Overhead Tangram pieces (optional)

Overview

Children make a variety of Tangram polygons, measure their interior angles, and find the sum of their angles. In this activity, children have the opportunity to:

♦ create and compare polygons

♦ measure angles in degrees

♦ identify interior angles

♦ discover the relationships between number of sides in a polygon and the sum of its interior angles

The Activity

If children have not had experiences finding the degree measure of angles, you may want to have children do the lesson called "What's Your Angle?" (page 86) before this one.

Introducing

♦ Make a shape with the two small Tangram triangles and the parallelogram, like the one shown.

♦ Have the children count the angles of the shape with you. Point out that it has six interior angles. Explain that any angle inside a shape is called an *interior angle*.

♦ Point out several angles which are not interior angles, such as the ones indicated with an arrow.

interior angles

♦ Have children make several more shapes and count the interior angles.

♦ Finally, ask children how they would find the number of degrees in each of the interior angles.

On Their Own

How can you find the sum of the interior angles of any polygon without measuring each angle?

- Work with a partner. Each of you pick any 2 or more Tangram pieces and make a shape that has the same number of sides but looks different. Record the outline of your shape.

- Measure the interior angles of your shape. Find their sum. Record it.

- Make two more sets of shapes. Each time, make sure the shapes have a different number of sides than the set of shapes you just made.

- Study your shapes and the data. Be ready to talk about what you notice.

The Bigger Picture

Thinking and Sharing

Have children post their shapes, grouping them according to their number of sides. Give children time to remove any duplicates. Label each grouping with the appropriate number of sides and the corresponding interior-angle sum.

Use prompts such as these to promote class discussion:

- How did you measure the angles?
- Were some angles easier to measure than others? Why?
- What do you notice about the posted shapes?
- What patterns do you see?

Writing and Drawing

Ask children to make three different convex polygons. Have them trace, measure, and record the interior angles and the sum of the angles. Then have them explain whether they think it is possible to predict the sum of the interior angles in a convex polygon. Have them refer to their tracings when explaining their answer.

Extending the Activity

Have children work with a partner to make a shape from Tangram pieces whose interior angles have the greatest sum possible. Then have then trace, measure, and record the interior angle measures and their sum.

Where's the Mathematics?

It is possible to use a protractor to find the number of degrees in each angle, but it is easier to use the Tangram pieces themselves. Children can use the 90°-angle of the square as a benchmark. The acute angles of the Tangram triangles are each 45°, which can be verified by putting two Tangram triangles together on top of the square.

Some children may have trouble deciding which angle to measure in a concave polygon. To help them, you may suggest that children use crayons or markers to color in the interior of the region after it is traced, then measure only the angles that are colored in.

Putting the 90° angle and the 45°- angle together gives the larger angle measurement of the parallelogram—135°.

Children may notice that the degree measures of all their polygons end in either 0 or 5. They may also notice that their shapes have only six different size angles, the smallest being 45° and the largest being 315°. This makes sense once children realize that the Tangram pieces only have the following angle sizes: 45°, 90°, or 135°. The following shapes are representative of what children might post.

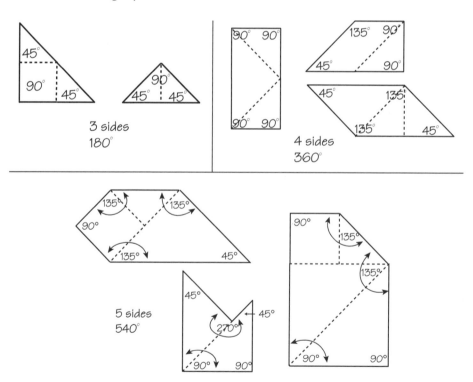

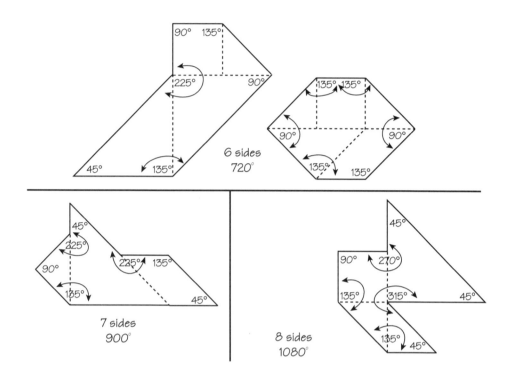

6 sides
720°

7 sides
900°

8 sides
1080°

Many children are surprised that the number of sides, not the shape of the polygon, determines the interior angle sum. All the polygons with the same number of sides have the same interior angle sum. Triangles have the smallest sum, 180°. Quadrilaterals, or four-sided figures, have sums of 360°. As the shapes get bigger, the number of degrees increases. In fact, every time a side is added, the sum increases by 180°.

This 180°-increment can be explained by partitioning a convex polygon into triangles. Pick a vertex. From that vertex draw a diagonal to every other vertex. The number of triangles formed is two less than the number of sides in the polygon. Since the sum of the interior angles of a triangle is 180°, multiplying the number of triangles by 180 yields the interior angle sum. For example, the hexagon, no matter what its shape, has an interior angle sum of 720° because it can be partitioned into 4 triangles, each having a sum of 180°.

A 12-sided shape (dodecagon) can be partitioned into 10 triangles; thus, the sum of its interior angles, is 1800°. An 18-sided shape has an interior angle sum of 2880°.

READY, SET, GO!

- Classifying
- Properties of geometric figures

Getting Ready

What You'll Need

Tangrams, 4 sets per group

Attribute Strips worksheet, 1 per group, page 93

Construction paper, 2 sheets per group

Overview

Children use Venn diagrams to sort and classify Tangram polygons. In this activity, children have the opportunity to:

- analyze and write properties of polygons
- use visual models to represent classifications
- explore the concepts of union and intersection of sets

The Activity

Children may want to use loops of string to make the Venn diagram at the table or on the floor and then redraw the diagram when all the pieces are in place.

Introducing

- Hold a Tangram square behind your back. Tell children you are going to give them clues so they can guess which piece you are holding. Give these clues: *Has at least one right angle. Is a quadrilateral.*

- After children determine that the hidden piece is a square, explain that the clues you gave them can also be called *attributes*.

- Draw a two-loop Venn diagram with the labels as shown below. Explain that the diagram can be used to classify and sort sets of objects. Tell children that since the square belongs in both sets, it should be put in the overlapping part of the circles, the space that belongs to both circles. Work together to place the other Tangram pieces in the appropriate sections of the Venn diagram.

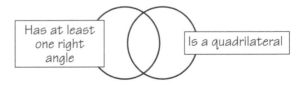

On Their Own

> ## Can you use a Venn diagram to sort Tangram shapes?
>
> - Make a group list of at least 12 attributes that describe the Tangram pieces or polygons made from 2 Tangram pieces.
>
> - Write each attribute on a separate Attribute Strip. Discard any strips that mean the same thing. Then mix up the strips and place them in a stack, face down.
>
> - Make a large Venn diagram like the one shown here. Pick 3 Attribute Strips from the stack, and tape 1 strip on each circle.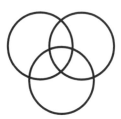
>
> - Now take turns placing your Tangram pieces or 2-piece Tangram polygons in the appropriate sections of the Venn diagram. Keep working until there are no different pieces or different polygons that can be placed.
>
> - Trace the pieces and polygons onto the appropriate sections of the Venn diagram.
>
> - Repeat the activity using 3 different Attribute strips.

The Bigger Picture

Thinking and Sharing

Post the groups' Venn diagrams. You may want to make a class list of the attributes that children wrote on their Attribute Strips.

Use prompts such as these to promote class discussion:

- How did you choose attributes for Tangram pieces and 2-piece Tangram polygons?

- Are some attributes too general? Give an example.

- Are some attributes too specific? Give an example.

- Which groups of attributes was the most interesting to work with? Why?

- When might it be possible to leave a section of a Venn diagram empty?

- Did your group always agree on where to place the pieces or the polygons?

- Did anyone find or make a polygon that did not belong in any section? Describe the shape.

Writing

Ask children to describe attributes for a three-circle Venn diagram whose intersection could not be filled with a polygon made from Tangram pieces. Tell them to explain how they know that there is no shape that could fit in the intersection of the loops.

Extending the Activity

1. Have children repeat the activity making polygons from two or more than two Tangram pieces.

Teacher Talk

Where's the Mathematics?

As children classify and then sort the polygons in this activity, their discussion of similarities and differences promotes understanding of both geometric shapes and the concepts of classification. Children also discover the importance of using accurate mathematical language.

In finding properties that are useful in sorting the polygons, children may discover that some may not be as helpful as others because they are too general. For example, "has straight lines" or "has angles" describes every polygon. Thus, neither attribute can be used to sort polygons into two or more sets.

As they gain experience, children may see the need to reword some attributes to make them more useful for categorizing. For example, a polygon that fits the attribute "has four right angles" can be further categorized whereas one that fits the attribute "is a square" cannot. Children may observe that the more general an attribute is, the more polygons they can find or make to fit it.

Here are some examples of attributes that children may write on their Attribute Strips:

HAS ONE OR MORE RIGHT ANGLES

HAS THREE SIDES

HAS NO RIGHT ANGLES

IS A QUADRILATERAL

HAS ONE OR MORE OBTUSE ANGLES

ALL SIDES ARE EQUAL

HAS ALL OBTUSE ANGLES

NO SIDES ARE EQUAL

IS CONVEX

HAS AT LEAST ONE SET OF PARALLEL SIDES

HAS AN AREA LARGER THAN THE MEDIUM TRIANGLE

HAS AN AREA EQUAL TO THE LARGE TRIANGLE

HAS A PERIMETER LESS THAN 20 CM

HAS ONE OR MORE LINES OF SYMMETRY

2. Have children play a game in which points are given for the placement of polygons, as follows:

Fits none of the attributes = 0 point
Fits only one attribute = 1 point
Fits in the intersection of two circles = 2 points
Fits in the intersection of three circles = 3 points
Misplacing a polygon = –1 point

This partially completed three-loop Venn diagram may be similar to the ones made by your class.

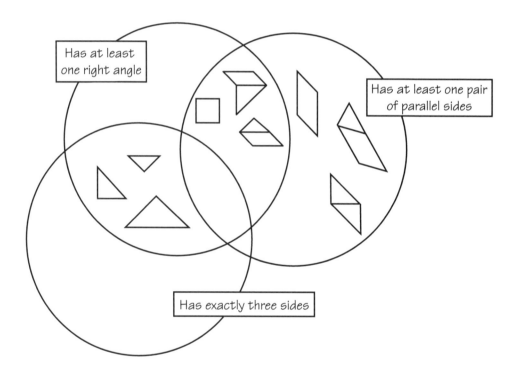

Children may observe that single Tangram pieces have specific attributes that limit where they can be placed in the Venn diagram. They may also realize that putting two Tangram pieces together makes it possible to form a polygon that does fit one of the attribute labels.

After completing this activity, children may suggest using Venn diagrams to sort and classify other types of information. They may also connect the use of Venn diagrams to outlining and organizing facts in history, social studies, and science.

SAME OR SIMILAR?

Getting Ready

What You'll Need

Tangrams, 4 sets per group

Tangram Tracing paper, page 94

Metric ruler, 1 per group

Protractor, 1 per group

Overhead Tangram pieces and/or Tangram paper transparency (optional)

Overview

Children build quadrilaterals from Tangram pieces and identify figures that are similar and those that are congruent. In this activity, children have the opportunity to:

♦ investigate the properties of quadrilaterals

♦ classify and sort figures according to their properties

♦ develop strategies to test for similarity and congruence

The Activity

Introducing

♦ Display the three different-sized triangles, the square, and the parallelogram from one Tangram set. Ask children which pieces are examples of quadrilaterals.

♦ Then have them choose any two triangles from their Tangram sets and use them to make either a square or a parallelogram. Have them trace and cut out their shapes.

♦ Ask children to place the cut-out shapes over one another to find shapes that are *congruent*, or match exactly. Then ask them to find some that are *similar*, or the same in shape but not in size.

On Their Own

Can you make and sort a collection of quadrilaterals?

- Share 4 sets of Tangram pieces. Each person in your group uses any pieces to make 6 four-sided figures, or quadrilaterals. Your quadrilaterals should include at least one of each of these shapes: a square, a rectangle, a non-rectangular parallelogram, and a trapezoid.

- Record the quadrilaterals on Tangram tracing paper. Then cut out the quadrilaterals and write your name on each one.

- When all the members of your group are finished, work together to sort the quadrilaterals into these categories: squares, rectangles, non-rectangular parallelograms, trapezoids, and others.

- Then look at each category and decide which quadrilaterals are congruent (exact matches), and which are similar (the same shape but not the same size).

- Be ready to explain how you made your decisions.

The Bigger Picture

Thinking and Sharing

Ask a group of children to show an example of congruent squares. Put one of the squares at the top of a large piece of paper. Make two columns under the shape: *Congruent* and *Similar*. Have other groups add their squares to the appropriate column of the chart. Repeat this process for rectangles, non-rectangular parallelograms, and trapezoids.

Use prompts like these to promote class discussion:

- How are the columns of the chart the same? How are they different?

- Which quadrilateral has the fewest shapes in the *Congruent* column? Why do you think this happened?

- How would the columns change if you put a different square, rectangle, parallelogram, or trapezoid at the top of the page? a different square at the top of the page?

- What strategies can you use to test pairs of shapes for congruence? for similarity?

- What is the least information you need to know about two quadrilaterals to be sure they are similar? to be sure they are congruent?

Writing

Have children tell how two quadrilaterals can be similar but not congruent.

Extending the Activity

1. Have children use the rectangles they made for the activity and ask them to draw a diagonal on each. Ask them how they can use the diagonals to test for similarity.

Teacher Talk   Where's the Mathematics?

There are a variety of quadrilaterals children can make with the Tangram pieces. Most children will find the squares, rectangles, non-rectangular parallelograms, and trapezoids. There are also some other quadrilaterals that can be made that have more irregular shapes.

The following is a portion of the class chart showing the trapezoid postings:

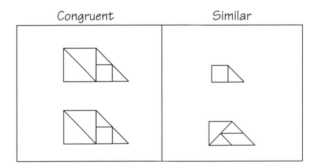

Children often have an intuitive understanding of congruence but confuse the term with similarity where shapes are enlargements or reductions of one another. As children build the set of quadrilaterals for this activity, their experiences and discussion will help to clarify and reinforce the meanings of the two terms.

To test for congruence, children may place their shapes over one another. Then they readily see when the sides and angles match exactly. It may not be as easy for children to recognize similar shapes. Some children may simply "eyeball" the shapes, deciding that any figures that "look the same" are similar. Other children are more exact and may choose to measure the sides and angles of shapes to check their observations.

2. Have children measure the side lengths of sets of similar quadrilaterals, record the data, and look for patterns. From the data, they should try to predict the measurements of a new member of the set, then draw that quadrilateral and test for similarity.

Children may be surprised to find that all squares are similar, but all rectangles are not. If they realize the proportional relationship between sides of similar rectangles and similar squares this may be more understandable. Experience with concrete models can provide a valuable, informal introduction to ratio and proportion. For example, children may observe that the side lengths of one rectangle are twice as long as the side lengths of another, making the two rectangles similar but not congruent.

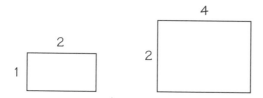

When working with squares and rectangles, children may note that it is not necessary to measure the angles, since since all the angles are right angles. They may also realize that they can use known angles in Tangram pieces to measure angles they are trying to check.

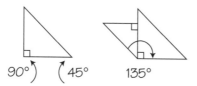

Children may observe that they have to make more measurements. They may note, as in the figures below, that for two figures to be similar, the corresponding angles of the figures must be the same and the corresponding sides must be in proportion.

As children explore similarity, they may draw on their knowledge of scale ratios. They may observe that maps, architectural plans, and scale models are similar, but not congruent to the real objects they represent. If you have not already done it, you may want to follow this activity with the Architan activity on page 18.

SHAPE SHIFTER

- Comparing
- Classifying
- Polygons
- Spatial visualization

Getting Ready

What You'll Need

Tangrams, 1 set per child

Die, 1 per group

Stopwatch or watch with a second hand, 1 per group

Overhead Tangram pieces (optional)

Overview

In this game for three to five players, children build shapes with certain numbers of sides from a given number of Tangram pieces. Players try to make the most shapes in the time allotted. In this activity, children have the opportunity to:

- ◆ combine shapes to make new shapes
- ◆ explore mathematical vocabulary
- ◆ use strategic thinking

The Activity

Introducing

- ◆ Ask a few volunteers to each choose two of their Tangram pieces and build a shape. Tell them to be sure that the pieces fit with no holes or gaps. Slide the shapes onto paper and trace around the outside of each. Then display the outlines to the class.

- ◆ Demonstrate how to count the sides of the shape outlines. Point out that, as shown here, one longer side is formed when smaller sides are aligned, and that added sides are formed when adjacent sides are not the same length.

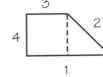

- ◆ Encourage children to use both formal and informal mathematical terms to discuss the shapes that have been formed.

On Their Own

Play *Shape Shifter!*

Here are the rules:

1. This is a game for 3 to 5 players. The object is to make as many Tangram shapes as possible before time is up.

2. Players take turns being the Timekeeper who:
   - Finds the number of Tangram pieces each player must use by rolling a die and adding 1.
   - Finds the number of sides that each new shape must have by rolling a die and adding 2.
   - Starts the game and stops it after 2 minutes.

3 + 1 = 4 pieces

4 + 2 = 6 sides

3. The other players:
   - Use Tangram pieces to make a shape that follows the Timekeeper's requirements and trace around the shape to record it. The pieces in the shape must fit with no holes or gaps.
   - Continue using their Tangram pieces or choosing different Tangram pieces to make and record all the shapes they can within 2 minutes.
   - Score 1 point for each shape that follows the Timekeeper's requirements.
4. The player with the most points wins.

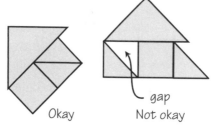

Okay   gap   Not okay

- Play *Shape Shifter* again until everyone has a chance to be the Timekeeper.

The Bigger Picture

Thinking and Sharing

Invite children to talk about their games and describe some of the thinking they did.

Use prompts like these to promote class discussion:

- What was the greatest number of shapes you made in one round? Why do you think you were able to make more that round than any other?

- How did you decide which pieces to use when you built a shape?

- What strategies did you use to build shapes with the correct number of pieces and sides? Did your strategies always work?

- Was it ever impossible to build shapes that met the requirements? Why do you think so?

- Which pieces do you think are easiest to work with? Which are hardest? Why do you think this is?

Extending the Activity

Have children play *Shape Shifter* again, this time scoring ten points for each convex shape and five points for each concave shape they make.

Teacher Talk

Where's the Mathematics?

The experimentation and problem solving involved in playing Shape Shifter develops children's spatial sense as they visualize and build polygons.

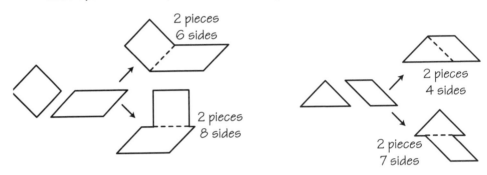

Children begin to understand characteristics of polygons (number of sides, number and type of angles) when they discuss and compare their results.

In the Shape Shifter game, many different polygons are possible. Children may discover that the shapes with four, five, or six sides are the easiest to build while some others are more challenging. Here are some shapes children may build:

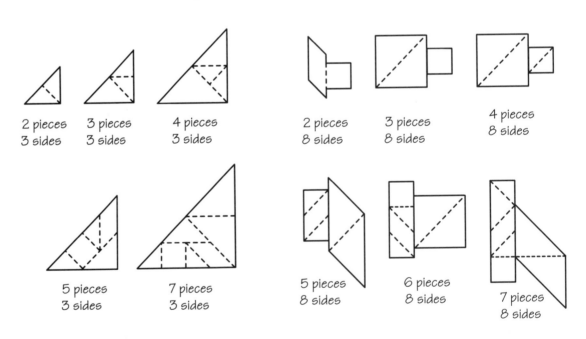

Some children may observe that there are no convex solutions with seven and eight sides and no concave three-sided polygons (triangles). They may also question one of the triangle solutions—the one made with six pieces—since it only approximates a triangle.

6 pieces
3 sides

As children build their polygons, differences in problem-solving strategies will emerge. For example, some children will find it easier to make adjacent sides congruent; others will prefer that adjacent sides do not match.

While experimenting, children have the opportunity to discover how Tangram sides can be manipulated. Some may find that two sides are lost when congruent edges of pieces are matched. If they do not want to lose two sides in their count, children can connect two adjacent edges that are not congruent.

Congruent edges
4 sides

Non-congruent edges
7 sides

Children may also note that some Tangram pieces are less likely to fit with others to form polygons. They may observe that piece selection is very important in some game situations. For example, to make an eight-sided polygon with two pieces, they must use the square and the parallelogram.

As they discuss strategies, children may begin to see how polygons that appear to be different may actually be transformations of the same polygon. Children may also see the importance of using exact mathematical language to make their viewpoint understood. For example, the term *trapezoid* is more specific than *quadrilateral*, and a large triangle with one right angle and two congruent legs can be specifically referred to as an *isosceles right triangle*. Mathematical language is more easily acquired when children have a need for it in order to complete the activity.

SQUARE COVER-UP

Getting Ready

What You'll Need

Tangrams, 1 set per child

Cover-Up Squares, several sheets per child, page 95

Overhead Tangram pieces and/or *Cover-Up Squares* transparency (optional)

Overview

Children cover a grid with Tangram pieces and find the percent of the grid that is covered. In this activity, children have the opportunity to:

- develop measurement and estimation strategies

- investigate percent spatially

- make connections between fractions and percents

The Activity

Point out that % is used to designate percent. For example, in 30%, the % symbol tells us that 30 is only a part of a larger group of 100, and that 30% can be expressed as the fraction $^{30}/_{100}$.

In On Their Own, *it may be helpful to allow children to estimate some of their answers, since some placements of Tangram pieces don't fit the grid exactly.*

Introducing

- Have children give examples of situations where they have heard the term *percent* used. List their responses on the board. Examples: a 30% chance of rain, clothes on sale for 50% off, a test grade of 95%.

- Discuss what percent means in the examples children give.

- Give each child a *Cover-Up Squares Worksheet* and ask children how many square centimeters are on one grid. Have children fit one set of Tangram pieces in the square. Point out that the seven Tangram pieces cover all 100 squares or 100% of the grid.

On Their Own

How can you find the percent of an entire area that shapes cover?

- Work in a group. Decide who will be the Percent Maker. Let everyone else be Percent Finders. The Percent Maker uses from 3 to 6 Tangram pieces to make a design that covers part of a 100-centimeter square grid.

- The Percent Finders copy the design on their grids. Then they count the squares to find the area covered by the pieces. For example, if the pieces cover an area of 25 of the 100 grid squares, then they cover 25 percent (25%) of the grid.

- When the Percent Finders agree on a percent, the Percent Maker traces the design and writes the percent on it. If the Percent Finders disagree on an exact answer, they may need to decide on an estimated answer.

- Repeat the activity until each person in the group has a chance to be the Percent Maker.

- Be ready to explain how you figured out the percents for each design.

The Bigger Picture

Thinking and Sharing

Have groups post their designs, arranging them in order from the least percent to the greatest.

Use prompts like these to promote class discussion:

- What do you notice about the posted designs and their percents?

- What strategies did you use to find the percent of a design? Which strategy worked best for you?

- In what cases did you estimate your answer?

- What is the greatest percent that can be covered with each number of pieces? What is the least percent?

- How could you use similar strategies to find the fractional part of the grid that is covered by a design?

- What arrangements of pieces did you find that covered the same percent of the grid?

- How are percents and fractions related? Give an example.

- How can you find the percent of an uncovered part of the grid?

Extending the Activity

1. Have children make a design with from three to seven Tangram pieces, trace it on the square grid, and give it to a partner. The partner should *estimate* the fraction and the percent of the grid covered. Then have the pair work together to find the exact answer and compare it to the estimates.

2. Have children repeat the activity using one Tangram set made up from two different colors. Tell them to write the percent that represents each of the areas. Then have them confirm that the three areas add up to 100% of the shape.

3. Ask children to repeat the activity using a grid that measures 14 cm on a side and can hold up to two sets of Tangrams. Point out that the new, larger square now equals 100%.

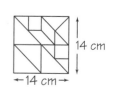

Where's the Mathematics?

Square Cover-Up gives children a visual model of how percents and fractions are related. Since the area of the square grid is 100 square centimeters (100 cm²) children can relate the area covered to a percent of the entire grid. As children measure area in square centimeters they begin to see, for example, that 50% of the grid means 50 of 100 squares and thus is also represented by the fraction ⁵⁰⁄₁₀₀, or ½.

Each of the samples below represents a different way that children may use Tangram pieces to cover a part of the grid. Yet, after studying these samples, children may be surprised to find that in each case the pieces cover one half, or 50%, of the grid.

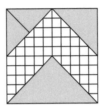 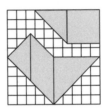 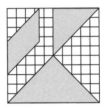 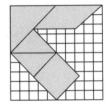

Thus, by sharing their completed designs, children see that there are many different ways to use Tangram pieces to represent the same percentage of the grid's area. They may also develop benchmarks for recognizing areas that represent specific percents such as 25%, 50%, and 75%.

As they realize that the number of squares covered is equal to the percent of the entire grid covered, children may use different strategies for finding the area covered by each Tangram piece. They may simply calculate the area of the entire grid by multiplying the length of the grid (10 cm) by the width (10 cm) and then use the knowledge that four large triangles make up the entire grid. Then, by dividing the entire area, 100 cm², by four, they find that the large triangle has an area of 25 cm².

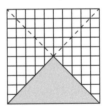

1 large triangle covers 25% of the grid

Children may also develop strategies for counting the grid squares. Some children may estimate a total. Other children may observe that partial squares often represent half of a grid square, and so may count each partial square as 1 and then divide by two to convert them into whole squares.

For example:

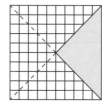

20 whole squares + 10 half squares

$$20 + \frac{10}{2}$$

20 + 5 = 25 whole squares,
or 25% of the grid

Children may also use what they know about the fractional relationship of Tangram pieces to find the percent of the square grid that each piece, or grouping of pieces, must cover. For example, since the Tangram set covers the entire square grid (100 cm²) and is made up of the equivalent of 16 small Tangram triangles, then the area covered by one small triangle is ¹⁄₁₆ of 100 or 6¼ cm².

Thus, the medium triangle, the parallelogram, and the square, which can all be covered by two small triangles, each have an area of 6¼ x 2, or 12½ cm², and the large triangle, which can be covered by four small triangles, has an area of 6¼ x 4 or 25 cm².

Knowing that a Tangram piece covers 6¼%, 12½%, or 25% of the square grid enables children to use addition to find the percent of any combination of pieces and subtraction to find the percent of any uncovered area.

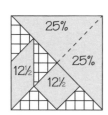

Since 75% of the grid is covered,
25% is uncovered.

Depending on their understanding of the concept of percent, you may wish to let children estimate and/or even "guesstimate" rather than allow them to become frustrated in their attempts to find exact percentages. In this activity, the methodology and the exactness of the solutions is secondary to the understanding that the Percent Makers and the Percent Finders are developing regarding the relationship of areas, fractions, and percents.

TAKE A BITE!

- Comparing
- Transformational geometry
- Spatial visualization

Overview

Children create squares that can be filled in a variety of ways with nine Tangram pieces—one Tangram set plus two additional small triangles. In this activity, children have the opportunity to:

- experiment with slides, flips, and rotations
- compare arrangements
- realize that different shapes can have the same area
- use spatial reasoning

The Activity

Introducing

- Have children set aside the two large triangles from their Tangram set.
- Ask them to make a triangle with any three of the remaining pieces.
- Ask volunteers to share their work. Most likely, children will have found the following:

- Establish that there are many ways to make the same size triangle.

On Their Own

How many different Take a Bite! squares can you make with your Tangram set?

- Work with a group. Place your Tangram set on an outline that looks like this. Position the pieces so that 2 spaces, each the size of a small Tangram triangle, are left uncovered. Think of each as a "bite"! Make sure you:

    - Use all 7 Tangram pieces.
    - Do not overlap the pieces.
    - Fit the pieces within the grid lines.

- Record your solutions on the *Take a Bite!* recording sheet. Compare them and look for patterns.

- Find as many different solutions as you can.

The Bigger Picture

Thinking and Sharing

Have volunteers, one at a time, describe their solutions and post or draw them. Continue until all the different solutions that children made are on display.

Use prompts like these to promote class discussion:

- What do you notice about the squares on display?

- Did you notice any patterns? If so, did they help you find new solutions?

- Were some pieces easier to use before others? Explain.

- How did you convince yourself that none of your group's solutions were the same?

Extending the Activity

1. Have children repeat the activity, but change the shape of the "bite." Direct them to use a "bite" in the shape of a square, parallelogram, or medium triangle instead of two small triangles.

2. Have children repeat the activity keeping one "bite" in the middle of the square and one in the corner as shown.

3. Have children create *Take a Bite!* puzzles. Select one of their solutions and record it by coloring only the uncovered bites on a *Take a Bite!* worksheet. Have children put their names on the back of both their puzzle and their original solution. Store the puzzles in one folder and the solutions in another, so that throughout the school year, children can solve each other's puzzles and check their solutions.

Where's the Mathematics?

This spatial visualization experience is similar to that of doing a jigsaw puzzle. Children have the opportunity to identify differences among the squares they make and find a way to keep track of them.

Children quickly realize that the placement choices for the two large triangles is more limited than for the two small triangles. Through trial-and-error, children can find the placements shown below. Looking at them more closely, however, children can see that starting with one arrangement produces the others by flipping, rotating, or sliding either or both of the triangles.

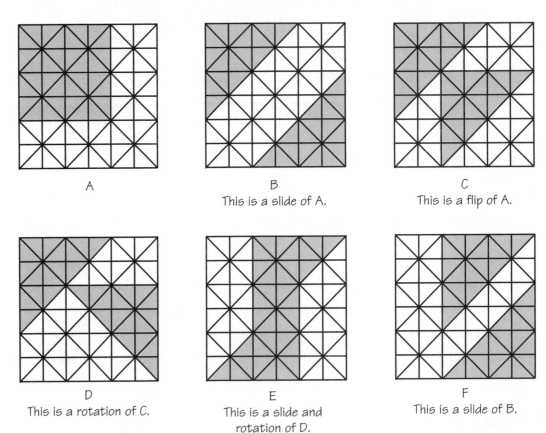

A

B
This is a slide of A.

C
This is a flip of A.

D
This is a rotation of C.

E
This is a slide and rotation of D.

F
This is a slide of B.

The two small triangles have the flexibility of being placed singly together and, thus, are best to leave to the end. Regardless of how they are arranged, the two triangles have the same area as the medium triangle, the parallelogram, or the square. Knowing that the two triangles can be made into a parallelogram helped to make this solution.

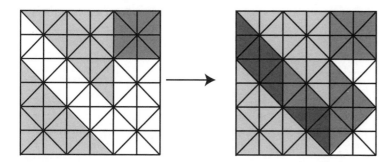

Some children claim that placing the parallelogram or the medium triangle is not easy and should be done as soon as the large triangles are positioned. Some children claim that trying to "be symmetric" helps.

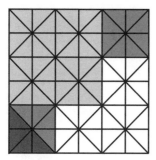
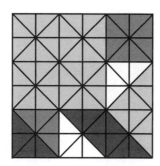

From a class discussion, it becomes apparent that there are many more solutions than those posted. Flipping or rotating different parts of a solution produces new solutions whereas flipping the entire arrangement does not. It is a challenge to determine whether or not one square is a transformation of another. All but one of these are different solutions.

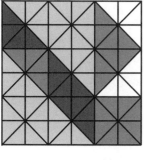
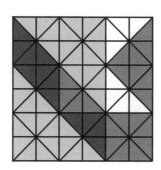
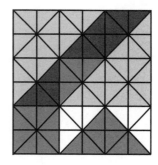

A   B   C (rotation of B)

This activity strengthens children's spatial reasoning skills as well as their ability to see geometric shapes within other shapes and different arrangements of the same shapes.

TANALOGY PUZZLES

• Comparing
• Properties of geometric figures

Getting Ready

What You'll Need

Tangrams, 4 sets in different colors per pair

Overhead Tangram pieces (optional)

The Activity

Before children begin On Their Own, point out that shapes in Tanalogy Puzzles can be made from one or more Tangram pieces.

Overview

Children use Tangram pieces to create analogy puzzles. In this activity, children have the opportunity to:

♦ analyze properties of polygons

♦ use logic and reasoning to classify polygons

♦ use visual models to represent analogies

Introducing

♦ Draw the following grid on the chalkboard. In the top row, write *hand* in the first box and *mitten* in the second. In the bottom row, write *foot* in the first box. Ask children to suggest a word for the remaining box.

♦ Explain that this linking of one thing to another based on a similarity is called an analogy. Say that this analogy is read as: *hand is to mitten as foot is to* ———.

♦ Have children suggest more word analogies. Discuss why there may be more than one right way to complete an analogy.

♦ Display this Tangram analogy, or "Tanalogy," puzzle. Explain that children are to choose a Tangram piece for the last box so that the relationship between the pieces in the bottom row is the same as the relationship between the pieces in the top row.

♦ Ask children to decide which Tangram piece is the best solution to the puzzle. As children make suggestions, have them define the rule, or relationship, they see in the top row. Accept all solutions children can justify.

©ETA/Cuisenaire®

On Their Own

> ## Can you make and solve Tanalogy puzzles?
>
> - With a partner, fold a sheet of paper into 4 boxes.
>
> - Make a Tanalogy puzzle. Start by placing 1 or more Tangram pieces in each of the top 2 boxes. Decide how the pieces in the left box are related to the pieces in the right box. Then choose more pieces that are related in the same way and place those in the bottom 2 boxes.
>
> - Record the pieces you placed in the top 2 boxes and the bottom left box. Then write or draw the missing piece or shape on the back of the paper. Write the rule you used to make the puzzle.
>
> - Trade puzzles with your partner, keeping them face up. Try to solve each other's puzzles. Compare your answer with the answer on the back of the paper. If you get a different correct answer, add your answer to the back and write the rule you used to find it.
>
> - Repeat the activity. This time, each of you should make 2 more puzzles.

The Bigger Picture

Thinking and Sharing

Ask children to post their favorite puzzles, pointing out the properties of Tangram pieces and of polygons made from them.

Use prompts like these to promote class discussion:

- What do you notice about the posted Tanalogy puzzles? How are they the same? How are they different?

- When you make an analogy, are you showing how things are the same? Are you showing how things are different? Explain.

- Did your partner ever find a different solution to your puzzle than you intended?

- Did you use certain Tangram pieces more often than others? Why?

- Does it matter which boxes you compare once all four shapes are placed in them? Explain.

- Which puzzles were easiest to solve? Which were more difficult? Why?

Writing

Have children make up word analogy puzzles that focus on the properties of shapes. For example, *Car is to tricycle as square is to triangle.*

Extending the Activity

Have children make larger Tanalogy puzzles by folding their papers into six boxes—two rows of three boxes each. Explain that in a larger puzzle, the pieces or shapes in one row of the puzzle go through more than one change. For example, a red triangle in the first box might change color in the second box and change size in the third box.

Where's the Mathematics?

As children create and solve Tanalogy puzzles, they investigate the logical connections among the physical properties of color, size, and shape.

Some children may begin their puzzles by choosing Tangram pieces randomly for the top row, then look for the rule or relationship to use in filling in the second row. Children who use this approach may say that it is harder to make a puzzle than to solve it.

Even when they succeed at making a puzzle, some children may have difficulty explaining the rule, relationship, or connection between the pieces. Searching for the words to explain the relationships they see helps children develop a greater understanding of geometric concepts and the importance of using correct vocabulary.

Children may use color relationships in creating their first puzzles, then use properties such as angles, sides, area, and perimeter in their subsequent work.

Here are some examples of properties that children may use and the puzzles that they may create. In the example below, the property used is *number of sides*. In the top row, the square has one more side than the triangle. Therefore, any solution must be a pentagon since a pentagon has one more side than a trapezoid.

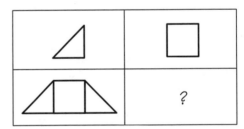

In the following example, *similarity* is the concept. The triangles in the top row are similar with their sides in the ratio of 1:2. Thus, the solution must be a square with sides twice as long as the one given.

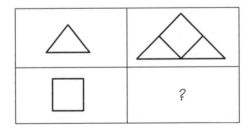

The property used below is *area*. In the top row, the large triangle has twice the area of the square. Thus, the possible solutions are the square, the medium triangle, the parallelogram, or any other shape with twice the area of the small triangle.

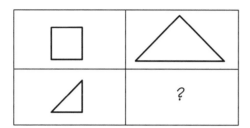

Children may be surprised that puzzles can have more than one solution. For example, in the puzzle below, if they follow the rule "The rectangle has the same height as the square but twice the base," then there are two ways to complete the puzzle. These are shown below the puzzle—a parallelogram with the same height and twice the base, and a trapezoid with the same height and twice the base.

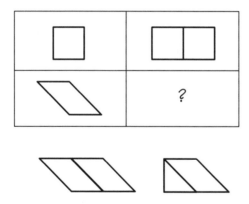

While making and solving Tanalogy puzzles, children are building and strengthening their logical thinking. You may want to start an Analogy Bulletin Board and have children post analogies they may make or find across the curriculum.

TAN-FASTIC!

- Estimating
- Comparing
- Properties of geometric figures
- Area
- Game strategies

Getting Ready

What You'll Need

Tangrams, 1 set per child and 1 additional set per group

Tangram Squares worksheet, 4 per child, page 98

Small Tangram Triangles, page 101(optional)

Die, 1 per group

Stick-on circles, 1- inch diameter (optional)

Overview

In this game for three or four players, children put Tangram pieces on a game board in an effort to be the first to fill a game board. In this activity, children have the opportunity to:

- ◆ estimate areas
- ◆ explore spatial relationships of polygons
- ◆ develop strategic thinking skills

If you roll a	Choose a piece or pieces with a total area of:
1	1
2	2
3	3
4	4
5	Remove a piece
6	FREE CHOICE! Choose any piece from the pile or from another player.

The Activity

You may want to use stick-on circles to label both sides of each Tangram piece with its area in small triangle units. The square, for example, can be marked this way. ②

Introducing

- ◆ Tell children to use the small Tangram triangle as a unit of measure. Then have them cover the Tangram parallelogram with small triangles. Point out that it can be covered with two small triangles. Measure each of the other Tangram pieces.

- ◆ Explain that in the following game children will put Tangram pieces on a game board according to the specific numbers of small triangles that can cover them.

On Their Own

Play Tan-Fastic!

Here are the rules.

1. This is a game for 3 or 4 players. The object is to be the first to fill a game board with Tangram pieces according to the roll of a die.

2. All players put their Tangram sets and an extra set together in a pile in the center of the group. Players take turns rolling a die. The number on the die tells them what pieces to place on their individual game boards. Here's the play for each roll of the die:

   If you roll...   What you do...
   - 1:   Choose a piece that can be covered by 1 small triangle.
   - 2:   Choose a piece or pieces that can be covered by 2 small triangles.
   - 3:   Choose a piece or pieces that can be covered by 3 small triangles.
   - 4:   Choose a piece or pieces that can be covered by 4 small triangles.
   - 5:   Remove a piece from your game board and put it back into the pile.
   - 6:   Free choice! Choose any piece from the pile or from any other player's game board.

3. If a player rolls a 1, 2, 3, or 4 and cannot make a play, the player rolls again.

4. On any turn, instead of rolling the die, a player may put a piece back into the pile OR may rearrange the pieces on his or her board.

5. The first player to fill the game board exactly wins.

6. After the game, all players record their game boards by tracing the pieces.

- Play 3 games of Tan-Fastic!
- Be ready to talk about your strategies.

The Bigger Picture

Thinking and Sharing

Invite children to talk about their games and describe some of the thinking they did.

Use prompts like these to promote class discussion:

- Which numbers rolled on the die gave you an easy move? Explain. Why?
- Which pieces did you think were the easiest and which were the most difficult to place on the board?
- Look at the game boards used by players who lost. Which piece or pieces were needed to win?
- Was it a good strategy to give up a roll and remove a Tangram from your board instead? Explain.
- Did you ever need to rearrange your Tangrams? Why?
- What winning strategies did you discover?

Drawing and Writing

Ask children to draw a game board that is partially filled with Tangram pieces, then trade papers with a partner. Then have children make a list explaining the die rolls, pieces, and moves a player would need to fill the partner's game board exactly.

Where's the Mathematics?

Tan-Fastic encourages children to experiment with the ways in which polygons fit together. Children may practice estimating areas and spatial reasoning as they explore game strategies.

As children combine geometric shapes, some randomly and some logically, they may begin to realize that the choice of pieces on each roll is an important part of their game strategy. For example, if a player rolls a 2 and there are no small triangles left, the medium triangle may be a better choice than the square or parallelogram.

At first children may think they should choose the largest pieces because the game board will fill up more quickly. They may discover that choosing smaller pieces gives them more options. For example, if a player rolls a 4, it may be more advantageous to pick 4 small triangles, or some combination of small pieces with an area of 4, rather than a large triangle.

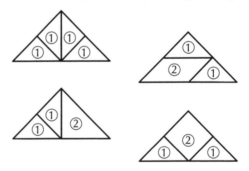

Some combinations of pieces
which can be covered by 4 small triangles.

Children may notice that good game strategy involves not only a careful choice of pieces, but the best placement of each piece, too.

Extending the Activity

1. Invite groups to design a new game board outline using exactly one set of Tangrams. Have them play *Tan-fastic* on their new game board. Ask children to be ready to explain how the new game board affects their strategies.

2. Have children play *Double Tan-Fastic*. Each child needs a double-size game board measuring 10 cm x 20 cm. Each group uses two Tangram sets per player, plus two extra sets.

The number of different winning arrangements depends on how many Tangram sets are used. However, children may discover that a winning game board has a total area of 16 units, and that if a board becomes "overfilled," a piece will need to be returned to the pile.

Here are some examples of winning game boards for two children using three Tangram sets.

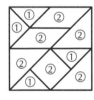

Adjusting to a changing situation adds to the challenge of this game. Children may use informal ideas of probability as they plan their game strategies. For example, it would be easy to fill the game board by rolling four 4's in a row and placing four large triangles. Children may observe that the chances of getting four 4's in a row are small.

As children evaluate the unfilled space and the remaining pieces, they may have to use a turn to completely rearrange the pieces on their game board. Children may better appreciate the variety of relationships among Tangrams as they rotate and flip pieces, exploring areas and angles.

TANGRAM RECIPE

- Polygons
- Spatial visualization
- Following directions

Getting Ready

What You'll Need

Tangrams, 1 set per child

Markers

1-Centimeter grid paper, page 91 (optional)

Overhead Tangram pieces (optional)

Overview

Children create a Tangram design and describe it in writing so that another child can read the description and duplicate the shape. In this activity, children have the opportunity to:

- ◆ analyze properties of polygons
- ◆ write about spatial relationships
- ◆ explore mathematical vocabulary

The Activity

Introducing

- ◆ Tell children that you would like them to follow a "recipe," or the instructions for building the Tangram design that you are thinking of.

- ◆ Then give your recipe. For example, for a three-piece Tangram sailboat you might say: Take a parallelogram, a medium triangle, and a small triangle. Place the parallelogram with the longer side going across. Then place the medium triangle on top of the parallelogram so that the sides match exactly. Place the small triangle to the left of the parallelogram so that those sides also match exactly.

- ◆ Draw this sailboat on the board, and have children compare their design with yours.

- ◆ As a class, discuss the challenges of the activity. Talk about which descriptive techniques worked and which did not.

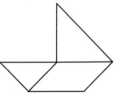

On Their Own

> ## Can you write a recipe for a Tangram design?
>
> - Work with a partner. Sit back-to-back or with a barrier between you. Each of you make a design using 4 to 7 pieces from your set of Tangrams.
>
> - Write a recipe for your design that your partner could use to make your design without seeing it. Use math terms, but write your recipe with the fewest possible words. Do not draw the design.
>
> - On another piece of paper, record the design, including its individual pieces. You will use the recording as your answer key.
>
> - Now exchange recipes. Try to follow your partner's recipe to build that design.
>
> - Then exchange answer keys, and compare the design you made to the one on your partner's answer key.
>
> - Talk about how the designs compare, and about ways to improve the recipes.

The Bigger Picture

Thinking and Sharing

When children have finished, have volunteers share their results. Discuss what was easy or difficult about describing or duplicating the designs.

Use prompts such as these to promote class discussion:

- Did all of the recipes name the pieces that needed to be used? If not, how did you know which pieces to work with?

- Are some pieces more difficult to write about than others? Why?

- When you used the recipe to make your partner's design, did the design match the answer key exactly? Why do you think this happened?

- Was there any part of your recipe that was hard to write? Give an example.

- Was there any part of your partner's recipe that was hard to understand? Give an example.

- How did you use the properties of a Tangram piece to help your partner know how to place the piece correctly?

- What makes a design easy to duplicate? What makes it more of a challenge?

Extending the Activity

1. Ask children to repeat the activity, this time using pieces from two Tangram sets to add color and complexity to their recipes.

2. Challenge children to repeat the activity using 1-centimeter grid paper. In this variation, they mark two axes, each from 1 to 15, and indicate ordered pairs to describe precise locations of the Tangram pieces on the grid.

Where's the Mathematics?

In *Tangram Recipe*, children attempt to write the most concise, accurate mathematical description of a design they can. In this way, children practice translating spatial relationships into math terms. As they write and follow Tangram recipes, children may place greater importance on learning mathematical vocabulary and recognize the need to agree on mathematical meanings and ideas.

To complete their recipes, children may ask to review such math terms as vertex, leg, base, angle, parallel, adjacent, hypotenuse, *and* trapezoid. *Children may also use informal language to describe these mathematical ideas.*

Children may find giving and listening to oral directions challenging, and they may notice that the most helpful directions are literal and precise. For example, the direction to "Put the triangle on top of the square" is not as helpful as "Center the long side of the medium triangle above the square."

When building their designs in the *On Their Own*, some children may choose recognizable figures (a swan, a house, a person), while others may make abstract geometrical designs. Children may not agree about which type of figure is easier to write about or easier to create from a recipe. Even if children build familiar objects, they may discover that not everyone interprets the parts of the object in the same way.

Here is an example of a design that a child might make and its recipe.

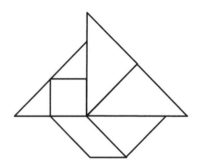

My design is a sailboat. The right sail is two large triangles joined along their short sides. The left sail is a triangle that is made from a square and two small triangles. To make the left sail, put a short side of one triangle on top of the square and put a short side of the other triangle to the left side of the square. The base of the boat is a medium triangle and the parallelogram. They are joined so that one short side of the triangle and the long side of the parallelogram match exactly and make a trapezoid. The trapezoid's smaller base is down.

Some children may have trouble finding the right words to describe their designs and might feel that the more pieces they use, the more difficult it is to write a description.

If children try to recreate the design from their own directions they may find either that they can simplify the recipe or add missing information. Children may also modify their designs if, after reviewing their recipes, they find them too hard to follow.

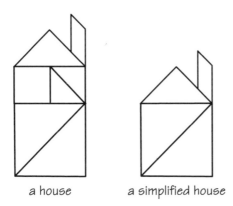

a house   a simplified house

Tangram Recipe can be repeated frequently to give children the chance to write and interpret oral or written directions for more complex designs. Here are a few sample designs that children might make that use all seven Tangram pieces.

THE MORE, THE BETTER

- Comparing
- Classifying
- Polygons
- Area
- Fractional equivalence
- Spatial visualization

Getting Ready

What You'll Need

Tangrams, 1 set per child

7-piece Tangram Squares, page 99, 1 per group (optional)

Overview

Children search for all the convex Tangram shapes that can be made with different numbers of pieces that represent the same fractional part of the seven-piece Tangram square. In this activity, children have the opportunity to:

- create and compare a variety of polygons
- recognize convex and concave polygons
- assign fractional amounts to each Tangram piece
- use equivalence
- work with fractions as an area model

The Activity

Introducing

- Show children a square made from the seven Tangram pieces.
- Tell children that the 7-piece square has a value equal to 1. Ask them to find the fractional value of each piece.
- Trace the square, showing the outline of each piece.
- As volunteers give the value of each piece and explain their reasoning, record the fractional amount in the appropriate place on the tracing.

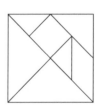

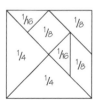

On Their Own

How can you make a Tangram shape that has a certain area?

- Work with a group. Each of you should make a shape whose area is ½ the area of the square made with all 7 Tangram pieces.

- Be sure that when you put pieces together they have no indents.

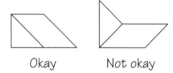

Okay   Not okay

- Compare your shapes. Record only those that are different.

- Count the number of pieces used for each shape.

- Make as many more shapes as you can that are also ½ the area of the 7-piece square, but each time use a different number of pieces. Find the least number of pieces possible, the greatest number of pieces, and all the possibilities in-between.

- Do this activity several more times. Each time, instead of ½, select one of these fractional amounts to be the area of your shape: ⅛, ¼, ⅜, ⅝, ¾.

- Look at your groups' solutions. Make a list of what your group observes.

The Bigger Picture

Thinking and Sharing

Discuss one fractional amount at a time. Have volunteers share the shapes they found and what they noticed.

Use prompts like these to promote class discussion:

- How did you decide which Tangram pieces to use for your shapes?

- How did you know your shape was the correct fractional amount of the 7-piece square?

- Were some fractional amounts easier to create than others? Which ones?

- Which fractional amount could be made in the most ways? Why?

- Which fractional amount could be made in the fewest ways? Why?

Extending the Activity

1. Give children the labeled Tangram square on page 99 or have them make their own. Show them how to represent the square with a number sentence such this: $\frac{1}{16} + \frac{1}{16} + \frac{1}{8} + \frac{1}{8} + \frac{1}{8} + \frac{1}{4} + \frac{1}{4} = 1$. Now have children write number sentences for each of the shapes they made when they did the activity.

2. Have children repeat the activity but allow concave shapes.

Where's the Mathematics?

As they build shapes whose areas are a specific fractional amount of the area of the 7-piece square, children deepen their understanding of equivalence. They also focus on a geometric attribute—convex vs. concave—often used to describe, identify, and classify polygons.

One-half of the area can be shown in more ways than any other fractional amount. And, while there is only one way to show one-half with two pieces, there are many ways to show it with five pieces. Children might start with the two large Tangram triangles, then make substitutions to make shapes with five pieces.

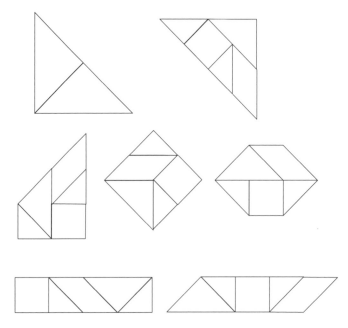

Some children think in terms of shapes only, such as 1 medium triangle equals 2 small triangles or 1 large triangle equals the 3 smaller triangles. Others use the fractional names of the pieces. For example, they will refer to the large triangles as the ¼-pieces, the medium triangle, the square, and the parallelogram as the ⅛-pieces, and the two small triangles as the ¹⁄₁₆-pieces.

It is not necessary for every group to have investigated every fraction before starting a class discussion. Here are some solutions for each of the other fractional amounts.

Shapes with ⅛ the area of the 7-piece Tangram square

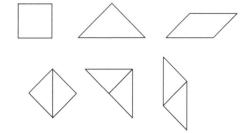

Shapes with ¼ the area of the 7-piece Tangram square

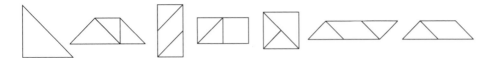

Shapes with ⅜ the area of the 7-piece Tangram square

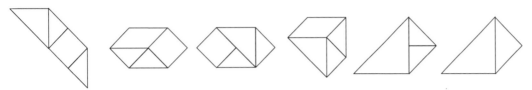

Shapes with ⅝ the area of the 7-piece Tangram square

Shapes with ¾ the area of the 7-piece Tangram square

Another way to focus on the data is to have the class organize the data in a chart like this.

	Number of Pieces					
Fractional Amount	1	2	3	4	5	6
½		✔		✔	✔	
⅛	✔	✔				
¼	✔	✔	✔			
⅜		✔	✔	✔		
⅝			✔	✔	✔	
¾					✔	✔

WHAT'S YOUR ANGLE?

- **Properties of polygons**
- **Angles**

Getting Ready

What You'll Need

Tangrams, 1 set per child
Overhead Tangrams (optional)

Overview

Children measure and name the angles of the Tangram pieces, then look for additional angles that can be made with two or more pieces. In this activity, children have the opportunity to:

- ◆ find the degree measurement of angles
- ◆ compare angles
- ◆ identify angles as *acute*, *right*, *obtuse*, and *reflex*

The Activity

Some children may point out that the hands of the clock form two angles. If so, help them identify each one as smaller than, larger than, or the same size as a right angle.

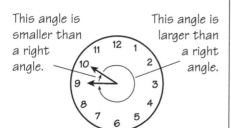

This angle is smaller than a right angle.

This angle is larger than a right angle.

Introducing

- ◆ Ask children what they know about angles.
- ◆ Establish that angles are measured in degrees, starting with 0°.
- ◆ Explain that a clock shows different angles throughout the day.
- ◆ Draw a clock face on the chalkboard showing 3 o'clock. Label the angle 90°.
- ◆ Have the children find the number of degrees when the clock shows 6 o'clock, 12 o'clock, and 9 o'clock.

- ◆ Then ask children to find the number of degrees in any five-minute interval. Confirm that it is 30°.

On Their Own

> ### How many different-size angles can you make with the Tangram pieces?
>
> - Work with a partner to find the degree measure of each angle of each Tangram piece. Record the information.
>
> - Identify each angle.
>
>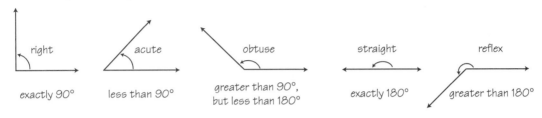
>
> right — exactly 90°
> acute — less than 90°
> obtuse — greater than 90°, but less than 180°
> straight — exactly 180°
> reflex — greater than 180°
>
> - Now see how many different angles you can make by putting two or more pieces around a point. Here's an example.
>
> $$\begin{array}{r} 90° \\ +\ 45° \\ \hline 135° \end{array}$$
>
> obtuse
>
> - Record each angle and its measurement. Identify each angle as acute, obtuse, or reflex.
>
> - Make a list of what you notice about the angle measurements you found.

The Bigger Picture

Thinking and Sharing

Have volunteers, one at a time, draw an angle that they found. Continue this until all possible angles have been displayed.

Use prompts such as these to promote class discussion:

- What do you notice about the angles that are posted?

- What kind of angles does the small Tangram triangle have? the square? the medium triangle? the large triangle?

- How many different angles could you find?

- Which angles were the hardest to figure out? the easiest? Why?

Extending the Activity

Have children find the sum of the interior angles of each shape they made and look for patterns.

Where's the Mathematics?

In this activity, children learn about the angles of the Tangram pieces. Only three different angles exist—90°, 45°, and 135°, *right*, *acute*, and *obtuse*, respectively. The square contains only right angles, the triangles each contain just one right angle, and the parallelogram contains none.

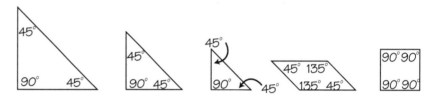

Many children are surprised that the triangles, which are different sizes, have the same size angles.

There are five additional angles that can be made from the Tangram pieces: 180°, 225°, 270°, 315°, and 360°. Each can be made in several different ways.

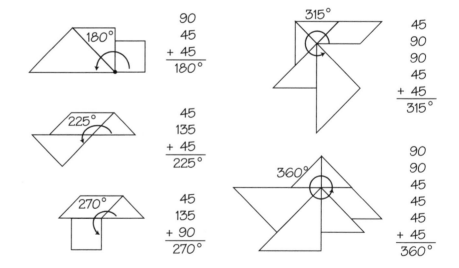

As they look at their data, patterns emerge. All the angles that can be made with the Tangram pieces end with a 0 or a 5. All are multiples of 45. The largest angle that can be made is 360° and the smallest is 45°.

Children justify that there are eight angles by trying two pieces, three pieces, four pieces, and so on. Some may notice that combinations of 360 can be made.

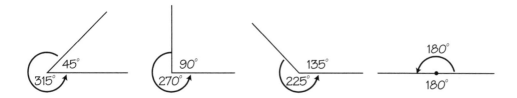

This activity helps children build mental images of a variety of angles. These benchmarks are especially valuable when children learn to use a protractor or must estimate the size of a particular angle.

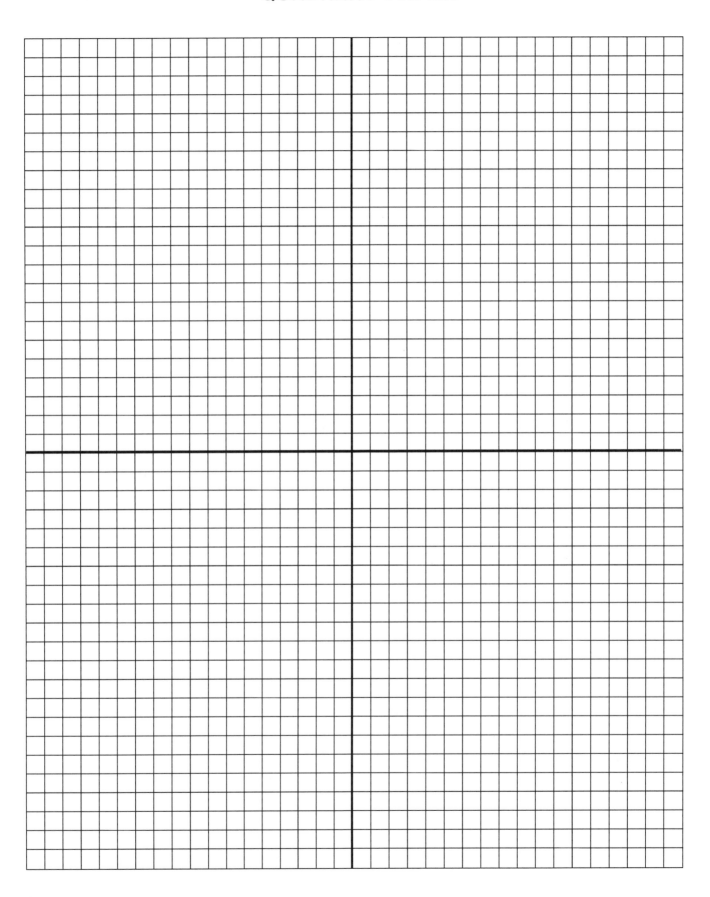

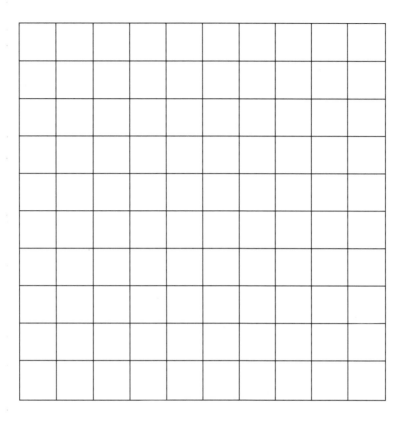

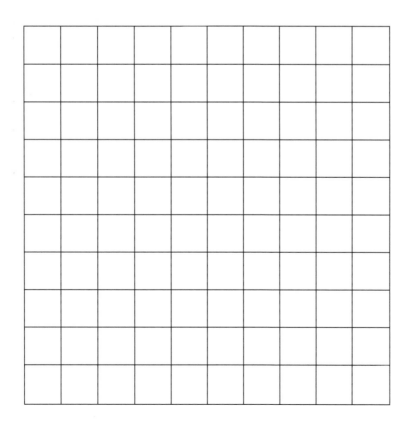

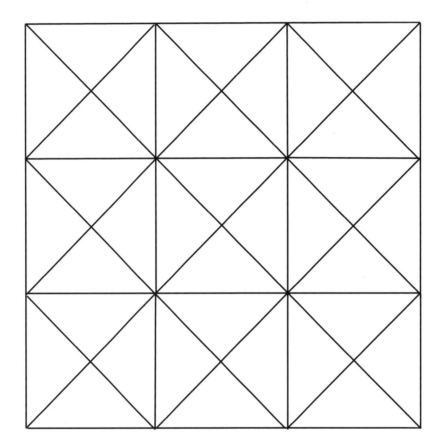

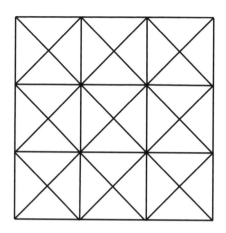

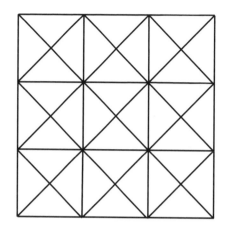

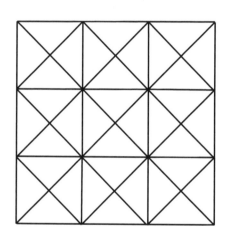

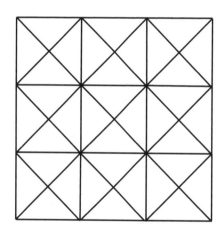

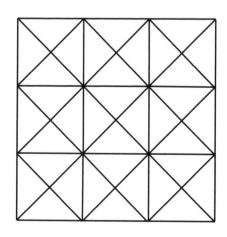

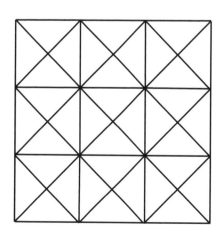

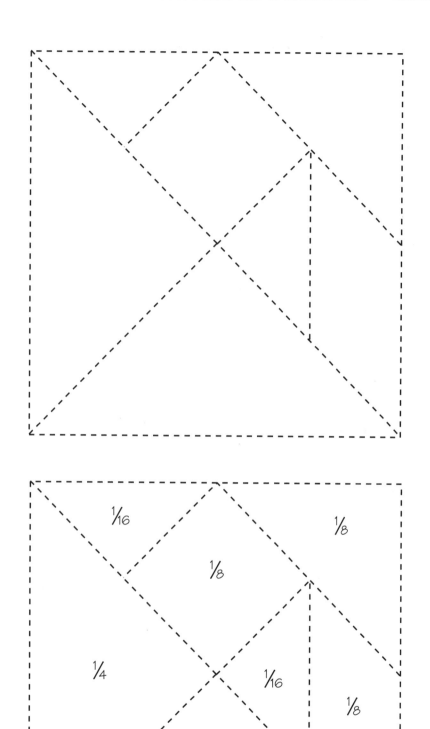

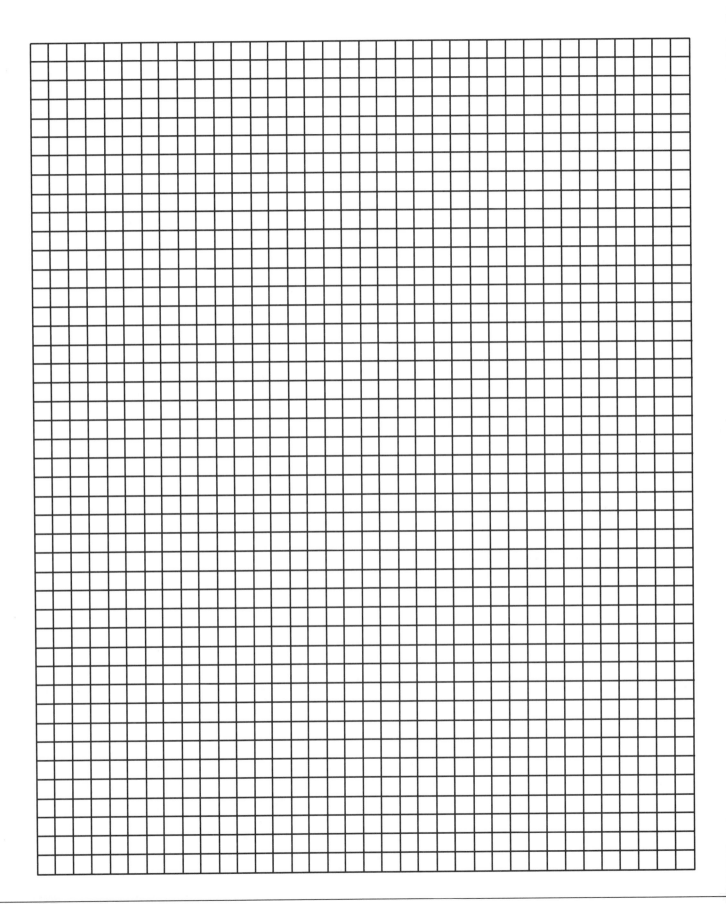

SMALL TANGRAM TRIANGLES

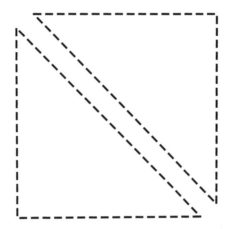

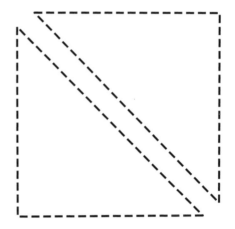

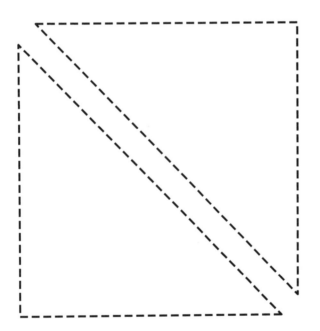

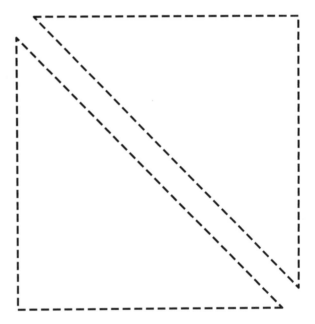

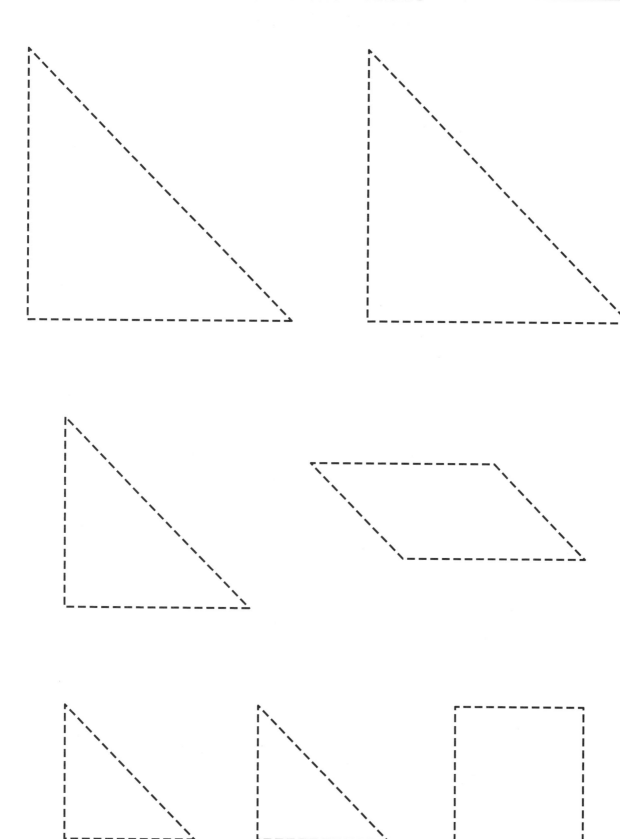